With the Naval Brigades in Egypt & Sudan

ADMIRAL OF THE FLEET SIR ARTHUR KNYVET WILSON, 3RD BARONET,
V.C, G.C.B, O.M, G.C.V.O.

With the Naval Brigades in Egypt & Sudan

Two First-Hand Accounts by Royal Navy Officers, 1882-85

ILLUSTRATED

How Wilson Won the V.C at El-Teb

Edward Eden Bradford

Extract of Memoirs of Charles Beresford

Lord Charles Beresford

LEONAUR

With the Naval Brigades in Egypt & Sudan
Two First-Hand Accounts by Royal Navy Officers, 1882-85
How Wilson Won the V.C at El-Teb
by Edward Eden Bradford
Extract of Memoirs of Charles Beresford
by Lord Charles Beresford

ILLUSTRATED

FIRST EDITION IN THIS FORM

Extracts first published in the titles
Memoirs of Admiral Lord Charles Beresford
and
Life of Admiral of the Fleet Sir Arthur Knyvet Wilson

Leonaur is an imprint of Oakpast Ltd
Copyright in this form © 2023 Oakpast Ltd

ISBN: 978-1-916535-60-2 (hardcover)
ISBN: 978-1-916535-61-9 (softcover)

http://www.leonaur.com

Publisher's Notes

The views expressed in this book are not necessarily
those of the publisher.

Contents

How Wilson Won the V.C at El-Teb

By Edward Eden Bradford

The condition of Egypt for some time past had been a source of much anxiety to the governments of Europe, and recently her affairs had gone from bad to worse. In May, 1882, there had been a "Revolt of the Colonels" headed by Arabi Bey, and on the 11th of June, a serious riot in Alexandria had caused much loss of life and damage to Europeans and their property, and a general exodus of the foreign population. The country was practically bankrupt and in rebellion.

The British Mediterranean Fleet and a French Squadron had assembled at Alexandria in May, where the forts were being repaired and replenished, and the Channel Fleet was ordered up to Malta. In these circumstances, the operations, that the *Hecla* had been intended to carry out with the Channel Fleet, were abandoned, and she was ordered instead to proceed at once to Malta. She made a fast passage out, and arrived there on the 1st of July. The Channel Fleet, under Wilson's cousin, Vice-Admiral Dowell, had already arrived, and were preparing to embark troops. One thousand marines were shortly expected in the *Tamar*, but there was no news of what action, if any, was about to be taken, and no one could see what the issue would be. As Wilson remarked:

> The government are making just sufficient preparation to irritate, but nothing approaching what is required if they really mean to attempt to coerce the Egyptians.

After a week of uncertainty he received orders to join the Admiral at Alexandria. Leaving that night (7th of July), Wilson, then aged 40 years and a captain, hustled his ship along at full speed the whole way, and arrived there half an hour before the bombardment of the forts began. He just had time to visit the *Sultan*, the senior officer's ship of the outside squadron, and get his orders before the ships opened fire.

7

A minute record of his observations of the events of this day, noted every few minutes as they occurred, has been preserved, with a diary of the principal events up to the 16th of August, but a more general account is furnished by the following letters:

Alexandria,
13th July.

Although by this time you probably know much more about what has been going on here than I do, you will like to have a few lines from me about Tuesday's doings. I played a very inglorious part in the affair, being merely a spectator. It was not a game that the *Hecla* was at all suited to take part in, so the admiral very properly kept me out of range. We got a splendid view of the whole thing, however, as I had nothing to do but to steam about just where I liked, keeping a little outside the distance at which the furthest shot seemed to pitch. It is not often one gets a chance of such a perfect view of an engagement without any risk. I thought the Egyptians showed a great deal of pluck. Until their heavy guns were actually capsized or disabled, they made a very good fight of it. They had in reality no chance of success from the very commencement, as only a few of their guns could penetrate the armour-plates of the ironclads, even under the most favourable circumstances, and all of these were very soon disabled.

In fact, no armour-plate was pierced at all, though the unarmoured parts were knocked about a good deal. Cabins suffered a good deal. I think in the flagship four of the cabins had shots through them, and the commander, having a shell burst right in the middle of his cabin, had all his worldly possessions reduced to chips in a moment. I could form no estimate as to the loss of life on shore, as they kept generally, of course, under the cover of the parapets, except when one occasionally got a glimpse of them at an embrasure while they were loading their guns; but the guns against them were so heavy and the shooting so straight, that I think they must have suffered heavily. I must say I was astonished at their showing fight at all. I thought that they would have abandoned the sea fortifications at once, as they knew we had no force that could touch them beyond the range of the ships' guns.

I suppose by the conditions under which Arabi holds his power

H.M.S. *Hecla*

he was obliged to try and show that the army was invincible, but he certainly made a great mistake. There is no inclination to show fight anywhere within range of the ships' guns now. Today the marines landed unopposed and took possession of the peninsula called Ras-el-Tin, which forms the outside of the harbour, and they are making their way to some extent through the town; but it is still burning, and I fear will be for some time to come a horrid scene of pillage and murder. I was in great luck to arrive in time, as I only got in half an hour before the action began. . . .

The next letter opens with a message to a friend, Mr. Amos, to confirm a telegram he had sent him about the destruction of his house and office. It then proceeds:

Alexandria,
20th July.

. . . We have had a period of almost incessant hard work since the bombardment, but no fighting. My work has been, first, spiking or disabling all the guns in the outlying forts, which cover an extent of 8 or 9 miles, and afterwards searching for magazines and destroying ammunition. I suppose the admiral thinks I have a good nose for explosives. There is an enormous store of ammunition in the principal magazine that I have been working a whole week to get rid of, but I am not allowed to blow it up, and I have to carry it half a mile to throw it into the sea.

Before order was re-established in Alexandria, I managed to get a large quantity of it carried down by the Arabs simply by sitting down in the middle of the high-road with three or four bags of biscuits and a few bluejackets to show what I wanted, and bribing the passers-by with biscuit to carry it down for me. Now, however, they have all flocked into the town, and I can get very little help.

Yesterday I came across an enormous store of torpedoes, which fortunately for us they did not use. Probably they did not know how. When I said we had not sufficient force I never considered the forts of Alexandria as coming into the question. I never thought they would show fight at all. Arabi has played our game in the kindest manner in the world. If he had only the sense to keep his men under cover and not fire a shot, we could never have landed with the force we had. I think, even if we did not mean to go on to Cairo, it was wicked to bombard the forts without a garrison ready to replace the one driven out. The whole of the pillage and murder and incendiarism which went on through Wednesday and Thursday night might have been saved if we had had a force on the spot to take possession as soon as the firing ceased.

The town is now perfectly safe, and both natives and foreigners are flocking back to it, but the question of the food supply must soon crop up if Arabi keeps the communication with the rest of Egypt cut off. We hear rumours of his men deserting him, and if so, things may settle down quietly; but if not, I can see nothing for it but a march on Cairo. . . . You will probably have seen by the papers that I lost one of my lieutenants by accidentally shooting himself. He is a very great loss to me, as he was a capital fellow. . . .

H.M.S. *Hecla*, Alexandria,
26th July, 1882.

I have had my hands very full of work, principally in destroying the Egyptians' powder and torpedoes, but they have such enormous stores here that it is a very long job. I have destroyed more than 1,000 torpedoes and at least 300 tons of powder. I think all the torpedoes are destroyed now, but there is any amount more powder. They have also converted the *Hecla* into a magazine, so that I have to keep all the other ships supplied with ammunition. I had an interesting little trip yesterday that gave me just a look at Arabi's outposts.

I was on board the *Helicon*, just going to luncheon with the admiral, when a message came from the general to say that there was a strip of land between Lake Mareotis and the railway embankment that Arabi might possibly advance by, and which his troops could not command, and asking if we could help him with any force on the lake. No one knew whether there was depth of water enough in the lake or not, but I offered at once to prepare a raft to carry two Gatling-guns, and to go and see what could be done. I then went back to my ship to start Norcock getting the raft ready, and then came back and went with Fisher to explore.

We got a truck and put two Gatling-guns on it in front of one

11

of the railway engines and started away down the line, until we found ourselves at the beginning of a causeway with a marsh on one side and the lake on the other, and could distinctly see Arabi's troops posted at the other end. They turned out in a hurry and lined their parapet but did not fire, and we had no object in firing at them. Fisher remained with the engine, keeping the guns bearing on them in case they attempted to advance, while I went down and waded about half a mile into the lake. The water, however, was nowhere up more than half-way to my knees, and even *Brandy* (his dog) who came with me could not find enough to swim in, so our scheme had to be given up.

We were so pleased with our armed railway-truck that we have set a party to work this morning to armour-plate it with some iron plates we found at the railway station, and sent word to the general that we had got an ironclad on the railway to defend him. One of the lieutenants of the *Invincible* has got charge of it now, and I think it will prove very useful if we ever attempt an advance from here.

We have no idea what they are going to do with regard to sending more troops. . . . In the meantime, Arabi has dammed up the canal so as to cut off our main water-supply, which will in a short time cause a great deal of misery in the town, though it will not affect us because we can condense.

William Dowell is round at Aboukir, very anxious to bombard the forts if he is only allowed. I saw him for a few minutes the day before yesterday. He had come round thinking the 48th had arrived with his boy Jack. They will not, however, be here till tomorrow probably.

Alexandria,
5th August.

I have been hard at work since I last wrote, partly in destroying powder, etc., partly in arranging for the supply of ammunition to our own ships, and latterly in mounting a 40-pounder gun on the railway, which I have today had an opportunity of bringing into action for the first time. I said in my last letter home, which I hope was forwarded to you, that Fisher and I had put our heads together and supplied the general with an ironclad truck armed with gatlings, which he was much taken with, and this led up to the idea of mounting a heavy gun in the same way. I had some trouble in persuading the admiral to let me try, as of course, as in duty bound, he foresaw all sorts of dangers and difficulties.

I first arranged it so that I could hoist the gun out and fire it on the ground alongside the railway, but that took more than half an hour, and in case of a reverse there was every chance of being cut off. So, I determined to try mounting it on the truck, so that it could be fired there. When I had got it ready yesterday afternoon, the general came out with me to see it fired, and as soon as he saw it, he said, 'Oh, it is sure to smash the truck all to pieces.' We fired two rounds and nothing happened, so he quite altered his opinion and went away delighted.

Today my gun was put in front of the train which took him out to fight, and I think on the whole did good service; at all events, nothing went wrong with the gun. As Arabi had pulled the rails up, and we had not time to lay them down again, I could not get nearer than 2,300 yards, and the enemy kept so well under cover that it was very difficult to tell what effect the shot had. I was firing nearly the whole time over the heads of our own men, so it was rather nervous work.

My heart was in my mouth once when one of the shots stripped and I heard it turning head over heels in air as it went along. Fortunately, it fell just beyond our men and hurt no one. I don't know in the least what the result of our afternoon's work has been. It has certainly shown that Arabi has a very strong position, and means to hold it. I don't think we can drive him out of it with our present force.

I thought the marines who were in front of me behaved exceedingly well; nothing could have been steadier than they were. The artillery fire opposed to us was very weak, only one shell pitched close to us, and then just as we thought they had found our range they left off firing, and I don't know what became of them. . . .

It is high time to go to bed now, as I want to be up at daylight to have another trip in the train to see that Arabi does not pull up any more rails. . . .

On the 10th of August, Sir John Adye arrived, and the diary records several distinguished visitors to see the new train.

. . . Our armoured train is in constant requisition, and judging from the number of Correspondents who come to see it, I think you will see full descriptions of it in the papers, and pictures as well in the illustrated ones. We go out every afternoon to see what Arabi is doing, but as a rule without firing. On Monday we wanted to find out exactly where his guns were placed, and as he sent out a long line of skirmishers to meet us, we fired a shot at them. It was a very bad shot, as we had misjudged the distance, and it went a long way over their heads, but the whole line of skirmishers disappeared like magic, running like rabbits into their holes. The shot had the desired effect, as all their guns opened fire, and rocket-batteries as well.

We just stopped long enough to note the positions of the guns, and then gave them another shot, a much better one than the first, and then moved off. In the middle of the night, I got a message from Fisher, to say the general was going to place some guns in a position he had asked him to occupy so as to prevent Arabi from pulling up the rails, but as he did not know how he was to get them across the canal, he had sent to Fisher to ask for help. We were to start with our train at six a.m., so there was not much time to spare, and I lay awake half the rest of the night thinking where I could lay my hands on any materials for building a bridge.

At four o'clock I collected four big packing-cases, some railway irons and planks in the railway station, and got away with our train half an hour late, but still before the soldiers were ready to start. On arrival at the place, we found a ferry-boat which with careful management could just be made to take the guns across, but the operation would take a long time, and the position would have been of very little use if they could not advance their guns quickly when they liked, so we decided to use the ferry-boat to get the guns across, but to build the bridge all the same. Fisher took charge of ferrying the guns, and I set to work to build the bridge, while the soldiers sat down under the trees and looked on.

It took us all day to build the bridge; the canal is 68 feet across— not quite as wide as the Cam, I should think. I was very well satisfied with its strength when it was finished, except that the mud is very soft and it may gradually settle down. The general came up just as it was finished, and was very grateful. I suggested to him that he ought to hire the ferry, as the poor old ferryman was quite thrown out of work by the bridge, and he promised to do so. We went out and had another look at Arabi last night; he has paid me the compliment of throwing up an enormous bank of earth across the front of the spot our 40-pounder was firing at on Saturday, which seems a sign that we did him some mischief. . . . I am inclined to think Saturday's business was a mistake on our part, as it has taught him his weakest points. . . .

H.M.S. *Hecla*, Alexandria,
14th August.

We have now got seven generals here, and not one of them has the most remote idea what we are going to do. It is to be hoped that Sir Garnet, who is due tomorrow, has the plans in his pocket, because we are simply wasting time now, and the worst of it is that Arabi is making the best use of his. . . . The troops are arriving fast, and the Naval Brigade, with the exception of two field guns and the armoured train, have returned to their ships, very unwillingly.

I should have liked them to have stopped until they had seen the inside of Arabi's present position, but I suppose in view of the possibility of trouble with France it is not thought right to keep the men long out of their ships. Possibly it may mean attacking Aboukir, which will gladden William Dowell's heart. It would be of no use by itself, but if done simultaneously with an advance either from this side or the Canal, it would make a very good diversion.

He thus foresaw the possibility of the stroke that was intended, but which was so well kept secret. Sir Garnet had not arrived, and in the meantime all these preparations at Alexandria were so much to the good. The letter continues:

Yesterday I had a little miniature battle of my own, which arose out of my work in destroying explosives. On Saturday I sent Norcock with a party of twenty-six men to burn a store of guncotton about 1½ miles outside our lines beyond Mex, Lord Charles Beresford, who knew the place, going with him. They burnt one store and were just ready for burning another when the outposts reported a large body of men advancing. They proved to be 300 or 400 Bedouins with some cavalry, and they were coming on very fast. Beresford and Norcock wisely decided that the best thing they could do was to retreat to their boats without firing, lighting the fuse to burn the guncotton before leaving. This burst into a furious blaze just as the Bedouins came up.

As I was at Ramleh with Fisher quite in the opposite direction, I only heard of this when I came on board in the evening. As there was still another store of guncotton to be destroyed, and worse, a large store of mechanical torpedo primers, just like Wilmot blew himself up with, that would most likely be used to set traps for us in front of their fortifications, I thought we ought to finish the job as soon as possible, so I went down to Mex as soon as it was daylight, roused up Beresford and Colonel Le Grand, who was in charge there, got two companies of marines and a 7-pounder gun and rocket, that Beresford had cleverly mounted on country carts, and sent them round by an inland road. We arranged that when they arrived at the place they were to be put as much out of sight as possible, and then Beresford was to show himself on the crest of the hill as a signal to me to land with the same party that were with Norcock on Saturday.

As we had to pass through a village, we thought most likely the villagers would give information to the Bedouins, and they would think we only had the same strength as before. The ground was very broken, being old quarries, so we had no difficulty in hiding our men, and as it was a strip of land about half a mile wide between the sea and the lake, we could command the whole of it. Well, we burnt the guncotton store, and then went to look at the store of primers. It was evident at once that some had been taken away. Norcock, being a careful man, had counted the cases overnight, so we counted them again, and found fifty-four missing. After a short search we found fifty in a ravine close by; four had been carried off, and they evidently meant to come back for the others.

We carried them all back again, and had just finished when one of the sentries reported horsemen advancing along the lake on our left, intended to let them come close up and catch them, but the impatient marines opened fire too soon, before I could get up and stop them; seeing them turn back, Beresford opened fire with his 7-pounder, and I believe knocked two of them off their horses, but they were soon out of range again. Then we saw the skirmishers on foot creeping round to the right and trying to come up behind a railway embankment that ran along the seashore, but two marines stationed to protect that part fired and turned them back. They kept dodging about, occasionally firing at us from behind different rocks, but at very long range, and the bullets nearly all fell short.

I stopped the firing on our side altogether in the hopes of drawing them on, but they were not to be tempted. In the meantime, Mr. McDonnell, the gunner, had burnt the store of primers, and the Bedouins gave it up and moved off. It was a very interesting day to me, but much more like a sham fight than a real one. . . .

> H.M.S. *Hecla*, Alexandria,
> 17th August.

. . . Sir Garnet was all yesterday holding a council of war, but nothing has yet transpired as to his plans. . . . You ask me whether the train is my invention or Fisher's. I am sure I cannot tell you, as almost every step has been the result of consultation between us; but the really hard work connected with it, which was persuading the authorities to let it be tried, is entirely his, as, of course, is all the responsibility. The plans for mounting and working the 40-pounder are mostly mine. . . .

> 18th August.

. . . At present we know nothing of Sir Garnet's plans. He is evidently a man with a mind of his own, who does not on these occasions take the world into his confidence. My orders are to be ready for sea at five o'clock tomorrow afternoon, and I have stores on board for Port Said, but that is all I know. I am leaving my gun behind on the train. I was told this morning to leave it for a crew of the *Invincible*, but I thought it was nearly as bad as giving it up to the enemy to turn it over to a strange crew, so I have now got leave to leave Davison and seven men behind, so that all the principal people will remain the same. . . .

The secret was not out yet, for the next afternoon and evening the ships in Aboukir Bay were surprised to see a long stream of transports arrive and anchor in the bay, and expectations ran high in the ships there of orders to land the next morning. It was only a feint, for by midnight every one of the transports had sailed for Port Said.

H.M.S. *Hecla*, Port Said,
24th August.

Since we came here and all the transports have passed up the Canal we know very little of what is going on. My little ship's company is a good deal scattered, so that I have representatives everywhere, but I hear nothing from them. . . . I have sent two torpedo-boats to Ismailia while I am here. The operation of taking possession of the Canal seems to have been exceedingly well done, and a great deal of fighting, as well as international complications, saved thereby. There has been a good deal of delay on account of transports running aground, but not more than was to have been expected, and as the Canal Company recovered from their sulks as soon as they saw that we really had possession, and put their pilots at our disposal, things are going smoothly enough as far as we can see from here now.

My first job on arrival was to lay the shore end of the telegraph cable from Alexandria, not a very warlike operation, but it entailed a good hard twenty-four hours' work for our men; then I thought we should have a very easy time of it, but last night some Arabs brought in a report of an intended attack on us from Fort Gnemih (?), about six miles to the west. As Fairfax, who is in charge of the place, was very busy, the admiral sent for me, and asked me to take charge of strengthening the defences on that side. . . . Fortunately, I had borrowed a horse in the afternoon, and had ridden over the ground and made up my mind what ought to be done, though with no idea then that I should have to superintend it, so I got leave from him at once to shift our lines outside the Arab town.

We landed shortly after eight o'clock with all the spades we could lay our hands on, and by ten we were comfortably entrenched, as the sand was easy digging, sentries posted, and the men stretched out; and, if they followed my example, enjoying a very comfortable sleep on the sand, which was almost as soft as a feather bed. . . . I am sorry to say that Fisher, who was my best and strongest ally, is down with fever. I believe he is getting better, but his ship is far off, and I cannot go and see him. . . .

The canal having been thus seized, notwithstanding the probable international complications that might ensue, the Navy ceased to take any share in the actual fighting, beyond landing a small brigade. The base of the Expeditionary Force was moved from Alexandria to Ismailia, and Lake Timsah, an open stretch of water in front of the latter town, became crowded with the shipping carrying the army and its stores. These were being landed with the utmost despatch under the directions of Captain Harry Rawson, and troops pushed forward to seize Kassassin, whence an attack could be delivered on the earthworks that the Egyptians were erecting at Tel-el-Kebir.

As soon as the congestion of shipping in the lake was relieved, the *Hecla* was directed to proceed there, and Wilson was ordered to take charge of that section of the Canal Guard, where the Bedouins had been giving trouble by "sniping" boats as they passed to and fro. He had two interesting guests with him for a few days, Colonels Redvers Buller, V.C., and Charles Warren, the latter of whom had come out to try and make use of his intimate acquaintance with the Bedouin tribes in discovering what had become of Professor Palmer and his two companions, Captain Gill and Lieutenant Charrington, who had gone on a mission to purchase camels in Arabia.

As he had landed a couple of field-guns for the defence of the town, he would not ask leave to go up to the front to see the battle, but he sent Norcock, the first lieutenant, up the Sweet Water Canal with a boat-load of guncotton, to destroy the dams that the Egyptians had made to cut off the water supply.

The Battle of Tel-el-Kebir was fought on the 13th of September, and on the next day he wrote:

> The wind-up of this business seems to have been exceedingly brilliant, as we hear today of Cairo being occupied and Kafr Dawar surrendering. . . . I have just had an account of the fighting at Tel-el-Kebir from Admiral Hoskins, who was up there, but you will see so much better ones in the papers before you get this that I need not detail it. The whole thing seems to have been well planned and well carried out. Poor Wyatt Rawson is, I am sorry to say, badly ill, and I fear is not likely to live. You will remember him as a small boy going for a pull in the skiff with us up to Porchester from the *Excellent* one afternoon. He has turned out a wonderfully good man in every sense of the word, and will be a great loss. . . .

On the 18th, he wrote again:

> I am re-embarking my guns and collecting my boats, and start

for Port Said tomorrow or next day. I have just got back from Tel-el-Kebir, where I went to see the battlefield, and I have come back much impressed by Sir Garnet's boldness in deciding to rush the lines in the way he did, and his skill in the way it was carried out. It seems to have been done exactly at the right time with everyone in the right place, which is very unusual in battles. I went up in my gig by the Sweet Water Canal, and slept on the bank at Kassassin, and got to Tel-el-Kebir about eight o'clock in the morning. We walked all over the lines some three miles or so in length, and it was well worth doing, although the heat, stench, and flies made it anything but pleasant. I jumped into the ditch and found it not very easy to get out again, even without anybody on the parapet to stop me, but I suppose our men helped each other up. . . .

Military operations ceased with the fall of Cairo, the *khedive* was able to return to his capital, and the services of the navy on shore were dispensed with. The ships, accordingly, collected the remaining scattered units of their men and guns, the Channel Fleet went home, and the *Hecla* sailed on the 26th for Malta, to go into dock and refit.

It is forty years (as at 1923), since these events occurred, and to quote a favourite phrase of Lord Fisher's, *the mountains of the future have become the molehills of the past*; but the negotiations which preceded these events had involved us in a long and bitter dispute with France, who had undeniable claims to a share in the restoration of the country. This, and the vested interests of Turkey and others, with the consequent restriction of aims and tentative measures, had produced an intolerable confusion, and our action in solving it was tersely described by Wilson a few months later, when commenting on the advice, "When in doubt, fight," given by Lord Alcester to his hosts on the occasion of a farewell dinner, he wrote:

To my mind, it represents the only reason there was for fighting. Matters had got so confused that it was necessary to fight to make a fresh start.

The events of the past two months could not but have had a lasting influence on the future thoughts and opinions of a man who had been so closely associated with them, and the letters which have been quoted in the last few pages are of particular value in indicating the opinion he had formed of the operations regarded as military measures, and as further displaying a remarkable fertility of resource, and a

10TH HUSSARS AT EL TEB

physical strength that knew no fatigue. Another feature is worthy of note. Though he had foreseen the possibility of a flank attack on the enemy's position from the canal, he had quite failed to guess Sir Garnet's intentions; but when these were developed, and their success was seen to have depended so much on the secrecy with which they had been guarded, he did not fail to express his approval. This experience was probably not without an influence in the development of that habit of reserve for which he was afterwards so much noted.

When the list of honours and rewards was published after the close of the campaign, it was observed that Wilson's name was not mentioned, notwithstanding the distinguished part he had played in its early stages; the following extract from a letter from Admiral Dowell to Wilson's mother is, therefore, inserted, to show what his brother officers thought of the omission:

H.M.S. *Minotaur*,
28th November.

. . . All naval men connected with the Egyptian business feel alike that Arthur has been very improperly passed over in the distribution of honours. An Egyptian or Turkish order, of course, he will get, but I do not take that into account. It was no surprise to me that his name was not among the C.B. list, for I had argued the matter out at the Admiralty before—of course it was no business of mine, as he was never in any way under my orders—but I had gone to Sir Cooper Key about two of the Channel Squadron . . . and I took the opportunity of asking what was to be done for Arthur, and was told 'Nothing;' but that they thoroughly knew what very good service he had done, and that he would be perfectly certain of having good appointments, but that his case in no way came within the Statute of the Order of the Bath.

Sir Beauchamp knew his value—his answer to me once when I spoke to him—'Do not I know Wilson? There is nothing I ever wanted him to do that he has not done, and done well;' and Captain Fisher, who is here dangerously ill, I am afraid did himself no good yesterday; he got so excited, they tell me, when speaking of Wilsons having been left out. . . . Arthur will benefit eventually; for the present, I fear you must be satisfied with the knowledge that his brother officers all feel that he merits the reward that he has not got. . . .

BATTLE OF EL TEB

The refit at Malta was completed in three weeks, and at the end of October, the *Hecla* was back again at that sink of iniquity, Port Said, where Wilson had the uncongenial task of preserving good order.

H.M.S. *Hecla*, Port Said,
24th October.

I was only one day at Alexandria, and then came on here, where I am now commandant with a garrison of 240 marines, who do both the garrison and police work until Baker Pasha can establish some sort of force, Egyptian or foreign, to take their place. I got myself into hot water with everybody in this country by giving a passage from Malta to a Mr. Broadly, who is the lawyer retained to defend Arabi. They are all so bloodthirsty they want him shot at once without a trial. I should like to shoot him, too; but there are so many other rebels in high places in England that I should like to shoot first, and, as rebels go, I think Arabi is rather a good sort.

At present all my time is taken up with questions of leases, and rent, and water rates, and rights of way, and such things. I am meddling, I need scarcely say, with things I know nothing about. Things that, for all I know, go off if you touch them; but the government have gone and bought a property here for £76,000, and there is no one here to look after it but the Senior Naval Officer. . . .

Port Said,
2nd November.

My reign will finish here about next Wednesday. I shan't be sorry to go. It is a remarkably dull place. If I had not got my torpedoes to play with, I do not know what I should do. We have got a population of about fifteen thousand here, mostly scoundrels I think, with a constant stream of drunken merchant seamen of all nations steadily flowing through to vary the monotony; but even with all that entertainment, the place cannot be called lively. The Marine Artillery make capital police and keep very good order. This week we have had a murderer to hang, all the Arab coal-heavers on strike, and the coal stores on fire, but even that doesn't make it interesting.

The Egyptian Governor governs the place, but as I have control of the garrison and the police, he cannot do much to enforce his orders without coming to me. We arrest all offenders and

Battle of El Teb showing the Naval Brigade in action

turn the natives over to him, and foreigners generally to their own consuls to be dealt with. At present I have had no trouble or difference with any of them. . . .

On the 6th, the *Invincible* arrived to take over these duties, and the next morning the *Hecla* started for Corfu and Fiume.

The purpose of his visit to Fiume was to witness the performance of a new pattern torpedo, and as soon as this was completed, he returned to Malta, and remained there for the rest of the winter. In February, 1883, after the carnival, he had gone round to Marsa Scirocco, at the south-east corner of the island, where there was more room and less distraction than in Valetta, to carry out some of his perpetual experiments with the torpedoes, when an incident occurred which afforded him an opportunity to carry out a smart piece of rescue work.

H.M.S. *Hecla*,
1st March.

. . .Yesterday forenoon a merchantship's boat came into harbour. As there was no ship visible from which she could have come, I sent a boat to find out where they had come from, and what was the matter. I found they had left their ship about sixty miles south-east of Malta in a nearly sinking condition, and that another boat had left at the same time, but they had seen nothing of her since. I telegraphed at once to the admiral, and got ready to start. I got the answer 'Go immediately' in about an hour's time, and in five minutes more I was off.

I thought from the account of the condition in which the ship had been left, about thirty-six hours before, there would be little chance of finding her afloat still, and there is no saying where a ship left to herself will drift to, so I could only make a guess as to her whereabouts and go zigzagging about, taking about fifteen miles each sweep.

We saw nothing till this afternoon, when we picked up the boat with the remainder of the crew, thirteen men, about fifteen miles further off from Malta than when they had left the ship. . . .As I had got all the crew, and it seemed hardly possible the ship could be still afloat, I gave up the search as soon as it got dark, and I am now on my way back to Malta. . . .

He was evidently pleased with his success in finding those men, for he referred to the subject again in a letter of a week later to announce his approaching return to England in the ship.

Captain Arthur Knyvet Wilson, V.C., R.N., at the Battle of Teb
from a sketch by our special artist, Mr. E. Villiers

The *Hecla* arrived at Spithead on the 31st of March, and after a short period at Portsmouth, was attached to the Channel Fleet for a course of exercises in mining and countermining at Berehaven.

The current idea of the day was that a fleet should be able to protect with its own resources any port that it might have to seize as a temporary base, and all heavy ships were supplied with a small outfit of mines and stores to afford the means of practice in peace, and, by the combination of several ships, provide the means to lay a minefield, or to countermine that of an enemy in war; but the use of these new weapons was far from being understood or practised, as Wilson in a previously quoted letter had urged that they should be. Torpedo lieutenants were still too scarce to allow of more than one to a fleet, and they had not enough influence to overcome even the inert resistance of an established routine.

It must, therefore, have been with particular satisfaction that he now received orders to draw up and submit a programme for such a course of exercises. He prescribed a full curriculum. First, a defensive system of observation mines in the fairway to and from the sea, with contact mines on either side of it, which was to be tested by the ships passing over it; then the construction and laying out of a boom, to be followed by the offensive operation of destroying it; of creeping and sweeping for the enemy's cables and mines; and, finally, of running lines of countermines.

Mistakes and faults were many. Mines were laid out of place and leaked, had to be weighed, repaired, and correctly laid, junctions were faulty and cables had to be "under run," the fault located and made good; but Wilson was the personification of patience in such circumstances, and eventually got it all right, and succeeded in giving a good demonstration of what could be done and how to do it.

Towards the end of November, 1883, the *Hecla* (a torpedo boat depot ship), returned to the Mediterranean, and after a short visit to Fiume to see Mr. Whitehead's latest improvements, proceeded to Malta.

Some two years previously, a revolt of the tribes in the Soudan had broken out under the *Mahdi*, and it had now reached proportions beyond the power of Egypt to suppress. An expedition under Hicks Pasha to preserve the provinces round Khartoum had been annihilated in November, and on the advice of the British Government, it was now decided to withdraw the garrisons, and to evacuate the country beyond Wady Haifa on the Nile.

The revolt had spread to the Red Sea littoral, where Osman Digna,

Osman Digna

a prominent slave-dealer at the little port of Suakin, who had been created *Emir* of the district by the *Mahdi*, had invested the two neighbouring Egyptian garrisons of Tokar and Sinkat. The *khedivial* forces sent to relieve them had been destroyed by the rebels, and it was not expected the two places could hold out much longer. A more determined attempt to relieve Tokar was therefore undertaken by Baker Pasha. With ten other British officers, and a mixed force of Turks, Egyptians, and Soudanese, he left Trinkitat, on the coast, about 40 miles to the south of Suakin, and on the 4th of February, was utterly routed at El Teb, the site of some wells about 11 miles inland. This disaster placed Suakin in danger, and a small force of bluejackets and marines was hastily landed from the ships there, to hold it until reinforcements could be collected.

The situation was critical, but on receipt of the news the British Government acted with laudable promptitude. A battalion of marines was sent out from home, regiments on their way to and from India were diverted to Suakin, and the marine detachments of the Mediterranean ships were ordered to be sent there. The *Hecla* was lying in Malta Harbour, and at 2 a.m. on the 8th of February, Wilson received orders to proceed at once with these 240 officers and men to Port Said. Leaving at 11 a.m. the same day, he reached Port Said on the 12th, transferred the marines to the troopship *Orontes*, and embarked in their place 170 men homeward bound from the *London*.

On the 16th he left Suez with a small tug and four water-tanks in tow, and after five days' constant trouble with these vessels and their tow-ropes, he sighted a ship on shore among the reefs, and at once stood in to her assistance. It was an uncharted coast, abounding in coral reefs, and needing great caution in navigation; but on finding the ship to be the *Neera*, with the 19th Hussars on board with 270 horses and mules, and the ship hard and fast ashore, he went close in, and proceeded to disembark them into his own ship and one or two other vessels that had come up.

While he was on board the *Neera* directing this work, the *Hecla* fouled her screw, and drifted on to one of the numerous reefs, but he quickly got her off by making sail. She was undamaged, and as soon as the screw had been cleared, he proceeded for Trinkitat, which he reached on the evening of the 23rd. By this time there had been assembled here a force of some 4,000 men under the command of Major-General Sir Gerald Graham, with which a further effort was about to be made to relieve Tokar, and efface the results of the previ-

The Naval Brigade at El Teb

ous failure. On the afternoon of the 28th, the expedition moved out to Fort Baker, and on the next morning continued the advance on El Teb, when there occurred the events described in the following letter:

H.M.S. *Hecla*, Trinkitat,
29th February.

I have just got back from a very pretty little fight, which you will have heard all about by telegraph long before you get this. I had no business there, but as I had nothing to do here, and the place where the battle was expected to, and actually did, take place was within walking distance, I thought I would walk out at daylight this morning in time to march out with the troops. We had sent twenty-five men with Conybeare and Henderson and a Gardner gun to represent the ship in the Naval Brigade, but I had nothing to do with that, and simply went as a spectator. I am afraid you will say I had no business to go, but it would not do to miss such a good chance of learning one's trade, and it was a most enjoyable day. I would not have missed it for anything, and as I was free to go where I liked, I saw all the best of it.

We went out in square, with all the impediments, including myself, in the centre, the Naval Brigade with their machine guns occupying the two leading corners. We could see the enemy in the hills in the distance before we had left Fort Baker more than about a mile, but as we approached, they all disappeared, and we saw nobody—nothing but two Krupp guns, which they had captured from Baker the other day, looking over a sort of parapet at us. We marched steadily past them, as if we were going to leave them on the left, and still we saw no sign of the Arabs until we were nearly abreast of the battery and 900 or 1,000 yards from it, when they opened fire with their Krupp guns and with rifles.

We marched steadily on without replying until we were right behind them, and had them between us and where we landed. Then we halted, and for some little time a sort of duel was kept up between the Royal Artillery with their 7-pounders and the Krupp guns in the fort, the naval machine guns occasionally joining also, but with no result of any importance on either side except occasionally a man or a horse being struck in the square; but most of the shots were kind enough to pass through without hurting anybody. When we had had enough of that the

Wilson fighting with his broken sword at El Teb

general gave the order to advance, and the men marched at first very steadily without firing.

At about 500 or 600 yards firing commenced, and then there was a frantic noise and shouting. Poor Lieutenant Royds of the *Carysfort* was shot through the body close to me and two or three men of the Naval Brigade, not, however, belonging to my own ship. I went on with the 65th Regiment, who were making straight for the battery of Krupp guns which had been pounding us; when we got within twenty or thirty yards a lot of the men broke their ranks and rushed ahead to get into the battery. The first man, however, had scarcely put his head over the parapet than back they all came, with about twenty Arabs with their spears close after their heels.

I stopped two or three and made them turn about, and one poor man said rather piteously, 'Don't stop me, sir, I am wounded,' and I saw he was wounded in the elbow. The greater part of the Arabs were shot almost instantly, but the rest came on without the slightest sign of fear. One of them tried to run his spear into the soldier next to me, but missed him. I tried to run him through with my sword, but it broke, and while my attention was taken up with this man, another came up and cut me over the head with a sword. Thanks to my pith helmet it only made a nice clear cut through the scalp, and did not hurt the skull; in fact, I hardly felt it afterwards. But the blood ran all over my face and clothes, and as water is too scarce in the desert to be used for washing purposes, I looked rather an object, and all my friends kept thinking I must be badly hurt.

I picked up another sword, but got no other opportunity of using it, though the Arabs came on in the most plucky manner. They would lie hidden in ones and twos under the scrubby bushes on little sand hillocks until we were within a hundred yards of them or less, and then they would spring up and run straight at us with their spears, of course generally to be shot before they had come far. They had any amount of rifles, and fired at us at long range, but they evidently thought the spear was the weapon for close quarters. They were certainly the most fearless creatures I have seen. One felt quite sorry such brave men should be killed, but there was no help for it.

If they only learnt to use their rifles in the same fearless way, they use their spears I don't think our men would have had much

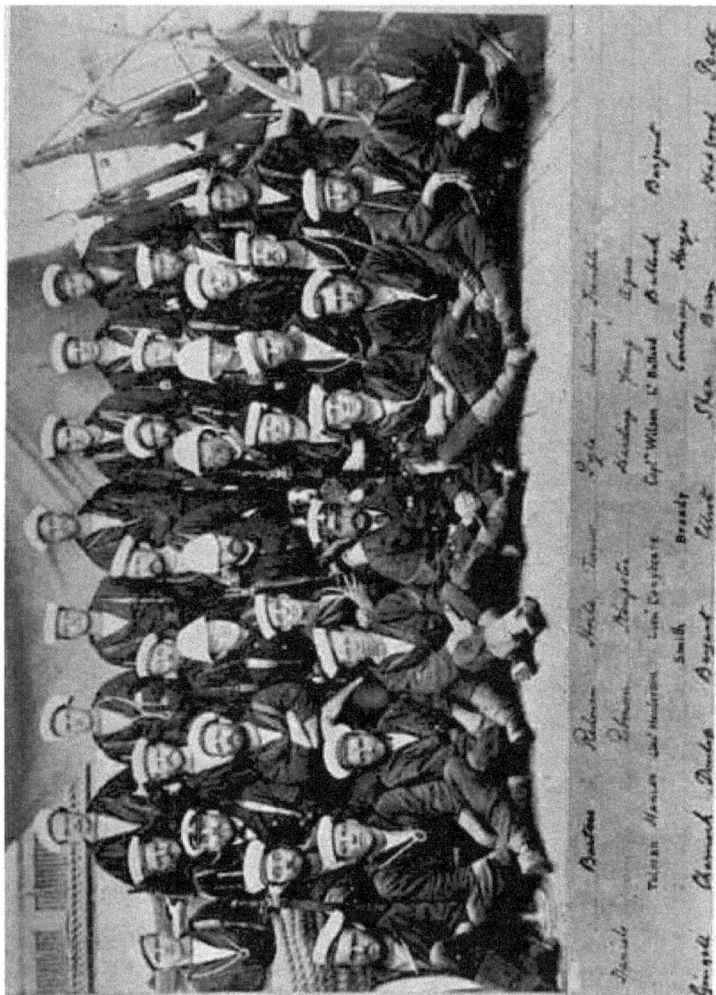

Captain Wilson and the Gardner Gun's crew, H.M.S. *Hecla* landed at Trinkitat and Suakin, 1884

chance with them. I came back to the ship in the afternoon and convoyed poor Royds, who was very badly hit, and as it was dark before we got back and the last part of the way was knee-deep in stiff clayey mud, it was rather a job for the men to carry him. My head is done up with sticking-plaster and is all right....

Such is his modest account of a very gallant personal action, performed in the course of a fight that was desperately maintained for three and a half hours. As far as he was concerned, with the return to his ship, and the writing of his letter to his friends, the incident was closed, and he dismissed it from his mind; but Redvers Buller, one of the brigadiers, had seen what occurred, having been just behind him at the time, and on the next day reported it to Sir Gerald Graham in an official letter as follows:

Teb

1st March.
I have the honour to bring to the notice of the Major-General Commanding the following distinguished act of bravery which came under my observation yesterday, which I would recommend as worthy of being submitted to the Lords Commissioners of the Admiralty for the distinction of the Victoria Cross.
Captain Wilson, R.N., of H.M.S. *Hecla*, on the staff of Rear-Admiral Sir William Hewett, V.C., K.C.B., attached himself during the advance on the Krupp battery yesterday to the right half battery, Naval Brigade, in the place of Lieutenant Royds, dangerously wounded.
As we closed on the battery the enemy moved out on the corner of the square and upon the gun detachment who were dragging the Gardner gun. Captain Wilson sprang to the front and joined for a second or two in single combat with some of the enemy, protecting his detachment till some men of the York and Lancaster Regiment assisted him with their bayonets.
But for the action of Captain Wilson I think one or more of his detachment must have been speared.
Captain Wilson was wounded, but remained with the half-battery during the day.

The press correspondents had also described the incident in their accounts of the action, but in more glowing terms than he had permitted himself to use, and embellished with certain fabulous details, so that the mail that carried back these accounts to the front, brought him a shower of congratulations and praise from relatives, friends, and old shipmates. He had already learned that he had been recommended for the V.C., but he took it all very modestly and coolly, and wrote to the captain of the *Vernon* his own version of the story, which, though it is largely a repetition of that already given, contains some details, and a statement of his view, which must not be omitted.

Off Suakin,
Friday, 21st March.

Dear Markham,

Thank you very much for your kind note, and will you also thank Durnford for his congratulations and the good wishes he sent me from the gunners and others of the *Vernon*. The papers have only arrived today, and I see they have been telling wonderful sensational stories about me. What really happened was this: When we got within thirty yards or so of the battery where the Krupp guns were, about a dozen of the 65th, evidently thinking the place was deserted, rushed forward out of the ranks, but they no sooner looked over the edge of the parapet than back they came with twenty or thirty Arabs after them. I stopped two or three of the soldiers, and made them turn round and face the Arabs, the greater part of whom were shot before they got to close quarters.

One fellow got in close to me and made a dig with his spear at the soldier on my left. He failed to reach him, and left his whole side exposed, so that I had a cool prod at him. He seemed to be beastly hard, and my sword broke against his ribs. The man on my right was a plucky fellow, and collared him round the neck and tried to throw him. The Arab still held on to his spear, so I hacked at him in a futile kind of way with the stump of my sword, and while I was doing so a second Arab came up and hit me over the head with a sword. My pith helmet took the greater part of the blow, so it only just cut the scalp, and I hardly felt it. Both Arabs were shot and bayoneted on the ground almost instantly.

If I could only have got a basin of water and washed my face, I should have escaped notoriety, but I only had a little cold tea in my water-bottle, and until we got to the wells there was no water to be got, so the blood ran all over my face, and the Cor-

SUAKIN—SOUTHERN HALF FROM THE SEA

respondents spotted me. General Buller, who was close behind, congratulated me in his cheery way, and he has since recommended me for the V.C. It has been a wonderful piece of luck, as I only walked out in the morning as a loafer just to see the fight.

The admiral has, however, since put me down as accompanying him. Nothing was further from my thoughts than going in for distinction of any kind, but as I happened to stumble into a hot corner, I could not possibly have done anything but what I did, unless took to my heels. . . . I have given you a long yarn about myself. I hope you will show it to anybody you think it will interest.

> Believe me,
> Yours very truly,
>
> A. K. Wilson.

On the rout of the Arabs, the expedition advanced, and reached Tokar the same afternoon without further opposition. The garrison having already surrendered, the civilian population were brought away, and on the return of the troops to Trinkitat, the whole force was embarked and conveyed to Suakin.

Sinkat had also fallen, but operations against Osman Digna, involving some hard fighting, were continued with a view to opening the route across the desert to Berber until, towards the end of the month, orders were received from England that they were to cease, and that the force, after providing a garrison for Suakin, was to be disbanded. During these few weeks the *Hecla*, unable to find room in the small and crowded harbour of Suakin, had been anchored about 12 miles off at the nearest suitable anchorage that Wilson could find, and from there had been sending her working parties daily to assist the work at the port; but with the conclusion of the campaign, her services were no longer required, and on the 2nd of April, having received the commendations of the admiral in a memorandum expressing his appreciation of the very able way in which Wilson had conducted the many trying duties entrusted to him, and his satisfaction with the behaviour of the officers and men, she left for Suez and the Mediterranean, and after calling at Alexandria, arrived at Malta on the 21st.

Extract of Memoirs of Charles Beresford

By Lord Charles Beresford

CHAPTER 1

The Beginning of Trouble

NOTE

The story of the Egyptian war may conveniently begin with an account of the affair of the 9th September, 1881, when Tewfik, *khedive* of Egypt, met Arabi Pasha face to face in the Square of Abdin at Cairo, and failed to take advantage of the greatest opportunity of his life. Had he acted there and then upon the counsel of Mr. (afterwards Sir) Auckland Colvin, British Controller, it is possible that the Egyptian war might have been avoided.

The beginning of the trouble was the jealousy existing between the native Egyptian and the Turkish, or Circassian, elements of the army. Rightly or wrongly, the Egyptian, or *fellah*, officers believed themselves to be slighted.

The Turkish, or Circassian, officers, being of the same race as the ruling family, regarded themselves as the dominant caste. In the time of Ismail Pasha, the predecessor of Tewfik, the Minister of War, Osman Pasha Rifki, a Circassian, perceived that his dignity was compromised by his being obliged to receive orders from the *khedive* through Ali Fehmi, captain of the Guards at the palace, a *fellah*. In the East, such a situation does not continue. Ali Fehmi mysteriously fell into disgrace. Naturally, he had a grievance; and he joined himself to two other officers of his race, who also had grievances. These were Abdel-el-Al and Ahmed Arabi, who was to become better known as Arabi Pasha. They were called the "Three Colonels," and to them came Mahmoud Sami Pasha, an exceedingly astute politician.

Arabi's particular injury was that he had been punished by Ismail for creating a disturbance under the palace windows, when he was

41

Charles Beresford. Admiral

one of the officers of the guard. Ismail had bluntly remarked that Arabi was more noisy but less useful than the big drum. Arabi joined a secret society of discontented officers, and shortly afterwards again fell into trouble under a charge of corruption while he was in command of transports during the war between Egypt and Abyssinia. Subsequently, Ismail allowed Arabi to join a regiment, whereupon he became chief of the secret society. One of its members divulged the secret to the *khedive*, who adopted the Oriental method of buying the allegiance of the disaffected officers by promoting in one day seventy of them to be lieutenant-colonels. He also presented one of his slaves to Arabi to wife.

So much for Ismail Pasha. When, by order of the *Sultan*, he was superseded by Tewfik, Arabi made haste to do obeisance to the new *khedive*, who made him a full colonel. But when Tewfik reduced the army, the Three Colonels presented a petition to the *khedive*, demanding, among other matters, that an Egyptian should be made Minister of War in place of Osman Rifki. The Three Colonels were thereupon arrested. Mahmoud Sami Pasha, a member of the Cabinet, secretly arranged that when they were brought before the court-martial, the soldiers should rescue them. On the 1st February, 1881, accordingly, the soldiers burst into the court, turned it inside out, and carried the Three Colonels to the palace. The *khedive*, confronted with physical force to which he had nothing to oppose, consented to supersede his war minister in favour of the crafty Mahmoud Sami, to increase the army by 18,000 men, and to abolish favouritism.

The *khedive* very soon discovered that Mahmoud Sami was by no means a desirable Minister of War, and also that the Three Colonels and their friends continued to stir up trouble. He therefore dismissed Mahmoud Sami and appointed in his stead the *khedive's* brother-in-law, Daoud Pasha, a Circassian, and ordered the disaffected regiments to leave Cairo. At the same time, it was rumoured that the *khedive* had obtained a secret decree from the *Sultan* condemning Arabi and his friends to death. When the order to remove his regiment from Cairo was received by Arabi, that leader of revolt informed the Minister of War on 9th September, 1881, that the troops in Cairo would proceed the same afternoon to the Palace of Abdin, there to demand of the *khedive* the dismissal of the Ministry, the convocation of the National Assembly, and the increase of the army. Then came Tewfik's opportunity, which, as already observed, he let slip.

When the *khedive* entered the Square, accompanied by Mr. Colvin, British Controller, and a few native and European officers, he was

43

Tewfik Pasha

confronted with some 4,000 soldiers and thirty guns. The following account of the critical moment is given by the Hon. Charles Royle, in his excellent history of *The Egyptian Campaigns*. (*Vide The Egyptian Campaign, 1882 & The Mahdist Campaigns, Sudan 1884-98* two books in one edition by Charles Royle: Leonaur 2013.)

The *khedive* advanced firmly towards a little group of officers and men (some of whom were mounted) in the centre. Colvin said to him, 'When Arabi presents himself, tell him to give up his sword and follow you. Then go the round of the regiments, address each separately, and give them the "order to disperse." the soldiers all this time were standing in easy attitudes, chatting, laughing, rolling up cigarettes, and eating pistachio nuts, looking, in fact, as little like desperate mutineers as could well be imagined. They apparently were there in obedience only to orders, and, without being either loyal or disloyal, might almost be regarded as disinterested spectators.

Arabi approached on horseback: the *khedive* called out to him to dismount. He did so, and came forward on foot with several others, and a guard with fixed bayonets, and saluted. As he advanced, Colvin said to the *khedive*, 'Now is the moment, give the word.'

He replied, 'We are between four fires. We shall be killed.'

Colvin said, 'Have courage.'

Tewfik again wavered, he turned for counsel to a native officer at his side, and repeated, 'What can I do? We are between four fires.' He then told Arabi to sheathe his sword. Arabi did so at once, his hand trembling so with nervousness that he could scarcely get the weapon back into its scabbard. The moment was lost. Instead of following Colvin's advice, and arresting Arabi on the spot, a step which would have at once put an end to the whole disturbance, the *khedive* walked towards him and commenced to parley.

The *khedive* subsequently agreed to dismiss the Ministry at Arabi's request; and Arabi thus advanced another step towards obtaining military control of the country. For a time, he prevented Cherif Pasha from forming a Ministry, and summoned to Cairo the Chamber of Notables. The members of the Chamber, however, whose office was purely advisory, supported Cherif Pasha. By means of a skilful intrigue, Mahmoud Sami contrived to obtain the appointment of Minister of

War. Arabi then effected a temporary retreat with his regiment to El Ouady, in the Delta, and waited upon events. It was then October. The *khedive* had convoked an assembly of the Chamber of Notables at the end of December, and in the meantime the elections were proceeding.

It should here be observed that Arabi did not merely represent discontent in the army. He had behind him a genuine and largely just popular agitation, the result of many evils suffered by the natives.

> Ismail's merciless exactions, and the pressure of foreign money-lenders, had given rise to a desire to limit the power of the *khedive*, and, above all, to abolish the Anglo-French control, which was considered as ruling the country simply for the benefit of the foreign bondholders. The control was further hated by the large landholders, because the law of liquidation (with which the Controllers in the minds of the people were associated) had in a measure sacrificed their claims for compensation in respect of the cancelling of a forced loan known as the '*Moukabaleh,*' and it was still more detested by the Pashas and native officials, because it interfered with the reckless squandering of public money, and the many opportunities for corruption by which they had so long been benefited.
>
> In addition to this, there was a great deal of irritation at the increasing number of highly paid European officials which the reformed administration inaugurated in the latter days of Ismail involved. The people began to suspect that what was occurring was only part of a plan for handing the country over to Europeans. The examples lately set by England with regard to Cyprus, and by France in Tunis, were, it must be owned, but little calculated to inspire confidence in the political morality of either of these two powers. (Royle.)

In these things consisted the reserve strength of Arabi; and while he was ostensibly in retirement at El Ouady (probably spending a good deal of time in Cairo with his fellow-conspirators), the native press continued to excite irritation against the Europeans; and when the new Chamber of Notables assembled on 25th December, 1881, they at once presented demands which brought the whole situation in Egypt to the notice of Europe. The Chamber demanded control of the revenues outside those assigned to the Public Debt, together with other new powers directly infringing the prerogatives of the *Sultan* and of the *khedive*.

It seems that Mahmoud Sami inspired these manifestations, not with any hope or desire that the demands of the Chamber would be granted, but because, as they were inadmissible, the Ministry of Cherif Pasha would be wrecked, and Mahmoud Sami thereby advantaged.

The British and French Governments declared that the demands of the Chamber were unacceptable. At the same time, they learned that the coast fortifications were being strengthened and that the army was to be increased. On behalf of the two Powers, a Joint Note was presented to the *khedive* in Cairo, on 8th January, 1882, stating that England and France were united in opposing "the dangers to which the Government of the *khedive* might be exposed."

The presentation of the Joint Note marks the beginning of that European intervention which might have prevented, but which did not prevent, the massacre in Alexandria of the 11th June, 1882, and which eventually resulted in the bombardment of that city on 11th July, 1882. The jealousy existing between France and England at that time in respect of intervention in Egypt, nullified the effective action of either party. Had M. Gambetta continued in power, he would prob-ably have forced Lord Granville to adopt a decisive policy. But M. de Freycinet, who succeeded Gambetta while the question was still un-der discussion, was as much afraid of responsibility as Lord Granville was. Diplomacy thus returned to its customary routine of addressing Circular Notes to the European Powers, and generally avoiding defi-nition as long as possible. Arabi seized his opportunity and announced that intervention on the part of England and France was inadmissible.

The Chamber of Notables also saw their chance, and demand-ed the dismissal of the Ministry. The *khedive*, apparently deserted by England and France, and much afraid of offending the *Sultan*, had no choice but to dismiss Cherif Pasha and to appoint in his stead Mahmoud Sami, who thus attained his object. Mahmoud Sami im-mediately appointed Arabi Pasha Minister of War. Arabi thus achieved a military dictatorship. It will be observed that his success was directly due to the vacillation of the English and French Governments. Mah-moud Sami at once forced the *khedive* to assent to the demands of the Chamber, and the English and French Controllers resigned, upon the ground that "the *khedive's* power no longer exists."

The dictators, Mahmoud Sami and Arabi (now Arabi Pasha), strengthened the coast fortifications, ordered ninety guns of Herr Krupp, and rapidly increased the army. Then the dictators, consider-ing that the hour of their vengeance had arrived, arrested fifty of the hated Circassian officers, (it is said) tortured them, and sentenced forty of them to perpetual exile. The *khedive* refused to sign the Decree; whereupon Mahmoud Sami threatened that his refusal would be followed by a general massacre of foreigners. A month later, on 11th June, such a massacre occurred.

In the meantime, the open quarrel between the *khedive* on the one side, and his Ministers, backed by the army, on the other, created general alarm. Mahmoud Sami convoked the Chamber; only to discover that the Notables were afraid to support him. Under these circumstances, Mahmoud Sami and Arabi Pasha informed the *khedive* that, on condition that he would guarantee the maintenance of public order, they would resign. The *khedive* replied in effect that it was not he but Arabi that troubled Israel. On the next day, 15th May, 1882, the English and French Consuls-General warned Arabi that in the event of disturbance, England, France and Turkey would deal with him. Arabi retorted that if a fleet arrived, he could not be responsible for the safety of the public. Upon the same day the consul-general informed the *khedive* that an Anglo-French Fleet was on its way to Alexandria, whereupon Mahmoud Sami and the rest of the Ministry made a formal submission to the *khedive*.

Such was the first influence, exerted from afar, of naval power. But when, upon the 19th and 20th May, the ships arrived at Alexandria, the effect was considerably lessened; for the force consisted of no more than one British line-of-battle ship, H.M.S. *Invincible*, with two gunboats, and one French line-of-battle ship, *La Gallisonière*, with two gunboats. The object of the Granville-Freycinet diplomacy, to do something and yet not to do it, had thus been triumphantly achieved.

The instructions given to the British and French admirals respectively are worth noting.

The British admiral was told to:

Communicate with the British Consul-General on arrival at Alexandria, and in concert with him propose to co-operate with naval forces of France to support the *khedive* and protect British subjects and Europeans, landing a force, if required, for latter object, such force not to leave protection of ships' guns without instructions from home.

It will be observed that Admiral Sir Frederick Beauchamp Seymour was not given enough men to form an efficient landing party; so that the futile clause concerning "the protection of the ships' guns" is hardly worth considering.

The French instructions were at least logical. The French admiral was plainly told to do nothing except in an emergency.

> On arrival at Alexandria communicate with the consul-general, who will, if necessary, indicate to you what you will have to do to give a moral support to the *khedive*. You will abstain, until you have contrary instructions, from any material act of war, unless you are attacked or have to protect the safety of Europeans.

Acting on the advice of the consuls-general, the *khedive* endeavoured to induce Mahmoud Sami and Arabi to resign. The dictators refused. The consuls-general thereupon presented them with an ultimatum, and the Ministry resigned; but the *khedive* was subsequently compelled by the threats of the army and the prayers of the terrified notables to reinstate Arabi Pasha. That leader at once published a proclamation stating that he guaranteed the public safety, which failed, however, to allay the public fears. On 29th May the European population of Alexandria drew up a memorial, which was telegraphed to the Foreign Office, stating that they were placed in extreme peril, against which the force at the disposal of the British admiral was totally inadequate.

Upon the same day, Admiral Seymour reported that earthworks were being raised on shore, and asked for reinforcements. On 30th May another line-of-battle ship arrived, with two gunboats, and three French warships. The rest of the British squadron in the Mediterranean were directed to cruise within touch of the admiral.

On the 7th June an Imperial Commissioner, Dervish Pasha, dispatched by the *Sultan*, arrived at Cairo. He was instructed to play a double part, the object of his mission being to counteract European influence. It was a complicated intrigue; but it is not worth unravelling, because Dervish Pasha presently discovered that the ruler of Egypt was Arabi Pasha.

Such is a summary of events up to the eve of the riots in Alexandria. At that moment, Arabi Pasha was military dictator; backed by the army and supported by popular sentiment: the *khedive*, still nominally ruler, was deprived of power and went in peril of his life; the *Sultan*, his overlord, whose dominant motive was the desire to avoid foreign intervention in Egypt, wrapped himself in diplomatic ambiguity; England and France, the only interested foreign Powers, each afraid of the other and both afraid of incurring responsibility, were in a state of miserable vacillation, for which (as usual) many helpless and innocent persons paid with their lives and property. In these circumstances, the advantage lay with the man who knew his own mind. That man was Arabi Pasha.

It seemed that nothing could better serve his ends than an organised massacre of Europeans by the populace, during which the police and the army should remain passive; for nothing could more effectually demonstrate the power of the dictator, bring the *khedive* into contempt, flout the foreign powers which had exhibited so contemptible a weakness, and delight the populace.

Accordingly, on Sunday, 11th June, 1882, a devastating riot broke out in Alexandria. The natives had been armed beforehand with *naboots*, or long sticks; the *mustaphazin*, or military police, joined in the attack; the soldiers remained immobile until Arabi telegraphed his orders from Cairo, when they at once stopped the disturbance. During the day, men, women and children, European and native, were shot, beaten, and murdered, and the town was looted. The loss of life was estimated at 150 persons.

In the evening the troops restored order, and subsequently maintained it up to the day of the bombardment. During that period, large numbers of persons left the city. Refugees of all nations were embarked in the harbour.

Lord Salisbury, who was then in Opposition, trenchantly exposed the true character of a policy whose direct result was that British subjects were "butchered under the very guns of the Fleet, which had never budged an inch to save them." The government had not given the admiral an adequate force. It was the old story of the naval officer being forced to subserve the ends of the politicians.

In England, public indignation forced the government to take action. The Channel Squadron was dispatched to Malta, there to remain at Admiral Seymour's disposal. Two battalions were sent to Cyprus.

Arabi Pasha brought more troops to Alexandria and continued to fortify the coast defences. In the meantime, the navy was helping to embark the refugees.

From this point, the general course of events may conveniently be related in the form of a diary, thus supplementing, for the purposes of reference, the detailed narrative of Lord Charles Beresford.

On 11th July the British Fleet bombarded the coast forts. The warships of other nations took no part in the action. The British force consisted of fifteen vessels and 5,728 men; eight ironclads, five gun-boats, a torpedo vessel and dispatch vessel. The forts were silenced and the gunners were driven from their batteries.

On 12th July the city was set on fire by the Egyptian troops. These, accompanied by civilians, looted the city and so departed.

On 13th July the British admiral landed 800 men. It will be observed that had Admiral Seymour been permitted to land a force upon the preceding day, he could have disarmed the Egyptian troops and prevented the conflagration. The *khedive* had taken refuge in his palace at Ramleh, and the *Condor*, Commander Lord Charles Beresford, was sent to lie off the palace to protect him. Captain John Fisher, H.M.S. *Inflexible*, was ordered to take command of the landing party. Upon occupying the outer lines, Captain Fisher, finding chaos in the town, in rear of his position, applied for an officer to exercise the duties of provost-marshal and chief of police, and suggested that Lord Charles Beresford should be appointed.

On 14th July the British force was occupying all important positions.

On 15th July Admiral Dowell, commanding the Channel Squadron, arrived in the *Monarch*. Lord Charles Beresford was appointed provost-marshal and chief of police to restore order.

Mr. John Ross, the British merchant in Alexandria who gave unsparing and generous assistance to the British forces—services for which he has never received recognition—writes to me as follows:—

Lord Charles Beresford saved millions' worth of property, causing the indemnity paid by the European Government to be much less than it would otherwise have been. I can assure you that there was a chance of the whole of Alexandria being burnt to the ground, had it not been for the wonderfully prompt, energetic, and scientific arrangements made by Lord Charles Beresford. . . I do not think England can ever be made to know properly and understand and appreciate enough with regard to what Lord Charles Beresford did for his country as well as for Egypt in 1882.

On 17th July 1,000, marines and 1,700 soldiers arrived. General Sir Archibald Alison took command of the whole of the land forces, now numbering in all, 3,686.

On the 20th July the British Government decided to dispatch an expedition to Egypt.

On the 21st July the water supply of Alexandria began to fail, Arabi having dammed the flow from the Nile into the Mahmoudieh Canal, and let salt water into it from Lake Mareotis. Hitherto the supply had been maintained by the gallant exertions of Mr. T. E. Cornish, manager of the waterworks. Sir Archibald Alison began his attacking movements.

On the 22nd July the *khedive* dismissed Arabi Pasha from his post of Minister of War. Arabi Pasha was now at Kafr Dowar with 5,000 to 30,000 men. A battalion of British troops sailed from Bombay.

On the 24th July Mr. Gladstone informed Parliament that the country was "not at war." On the same day the British troops occupied Ramleh, a suburb of Alexandria.

At this time Captain Fisher fitted out the armoured train.

On the 30th July the Scots Guards sailed for Alexandria. From the beginning to end of the war, there were dispatched, or under orders, from Great Britain and Mediterranean stations, 1,290 officers and 32,000 men. Add the Indian contingent, 170 officers, 7,100 men, consisting of 1st Seaforths, 1st Manchester, 1 Bombay and 2 Bengal battalions Native Infantry, 3 regiments Bengal Cavalry, 1 field battery, 1 mountain battery, and a section of Madras Sappers and Miners. Add to these, 3,500 followers, 1,700 horses, 840 ponies, 5,000 mules.

On the 1st August Lord Charles Beresford, having in the space of a fortnight saved the town of Alexandria from destruction and restored complete order, was relieved by Major Gordon.

On the 2nd August Admiral Sir William Hewett, with six vessels of war, occupied Suez.

On 3rd August the National Council declared its support of Arabi Pasha.

On 5th August General Alison attacked and defeated the enemy on the Mahmoudieh Canal.

On the 7th August the *khedive* issued a proclamation directed against Arabi Pasha and rebellion.

On the 10th August Sir John Adye, chief of staff, with the Duke of Connaught, arrived at Alexandria.

On the 12th August the Brigade of Guards, the Duke of Connaught at their head, marched through Alexandria to Ramleh, greatly impressing the populace.

On the 15th, General Commanding-in-Chief Sir Garnet Wolseley and Major-General Sir Evelyn Wood arrived at Alexandria.

On the 18th August the greater part of the troops embarked for

Port Said, the transports being escorted by five ironclads.

On the night of the 19th–20th August the navy took entire possession of the Suez Canal. The *Monarch* and *Iris* took Port Said. The *Orion, Northumberland, Carysfort* and *Coquette* took Ismailia. Admiral Hewett had already seized Suez.

On the 20th of August the troops and warships from Alexandria arrived at Port Said, together with Admiral Sir Beauchamp Seymour in the *Helicon*. M. Ferdinand de Lesseps had done his utmost to prevent the seizure of the Canal, which, he insisted, was neutral. It is said that when the troops began to disembark at Ismailia, M. de Lesseps, erect upon the landing-place, announced that "no one should land except over his dead body"; to which defiance a bluejacket, gently urging aside the heroic engineer, replied, "We don't want any dead bodies about here, sir; all you've got to do is to step back a bit" (Royle).

On the 21st August Sir Garnet Wolseley arrived at Ismailia in the *Salamis*, and, by orders of the *khedive*, issued a proclamation announcing that the sole object of Her Majesty's Government was "to re-establish the authority of the *khedive*."

The advance into the Delta was begun.

On the 24th August Wolseley captured the dam on the Fresh Water Canal.

On the 25th August the enemy were driven back upon Tel-el-Kebir. Mahmoud Fehmi Pasha, one of the original "Three Colonels," now Arabi's chief of staff, was captured at Mahsameh railway station.

On the 28th August occurred the action at Kassassin, in which the Egyptians were defeated. Kassassin was occupied. During the next few days men and stores were assembled there.

On the 9th September Arabi attacked Kassassin in force and was driven back to Tel-el-Kebir. Sir Garnet Wolseley made Kassassin his headquarters.

On the 12th September the army was concentrated at Kassassin. On that night the troops advanced towards Tel-el-Kebir.

On the 13th September an attack at dawn was made in three places upon the Egyptian entrenchments. The British carried them under a heavy fire at the point of the bayonet. The action was decisive. Arabi's power was broken. Arabi fled to Cairo.

The 6th Bengal Cavalry captured Zag-a-Zig the same evening; and the Cavalry division occupied Belbeis.

On 14th August the Cavalry Division rode from Belbeis to Cairo, starting at dawn and arriving at Abbassieh at 4.45 p.m. The same night,

NAVAL BRIGADE IN ALEXANDRIA 1882

Captain Watson, R.E., disarmed the troops in the Citadel and occupied Cairo.

On the 15th August Sir Garnet Wolseley and the Guards arrived at Cairo, a day before scheduled time.

During the next week, Kafr Dowar, a place of equal importance with Tel-el-Kebir, Aboukir, Rosetta and Damietta, surrendered.

From the bombardment of Alexandria to the capture of Cairo was sixty-six days, of which the campaign occupied twenty-five days.

On the 25th September the *khedive* returned to Cairo, where the greater number of the British troops assembled. Subsequently, Admiral Sir Beauchamp Seymour and Sir Garnet Wolseley were created Peers of the United Kingdom.

Arabi Pasha was tried by court-martial on a charge of rebellion against the *khedive*, and was condemned to death, the sentence being commuted to exile for life. In December, Arabi and six of his friends who had been sentenced sailed for Ceylon.

THE WAR IN EGYPT, BLUEJACKETS MOVING A CAPTURED SEVEN-INCH GUN FROM THE RAS-EL-TIN FORTS

CHAPTER 2

The Bombardment of Alexandria

My appointment to H.M.S. *Condor* was dated 31st December, 1881. The *Condor* was a single-screw composite sloop gun-vessel of 780 tons and 770 h.p., carrying one 4½-ton gun amidships, one 64-pr. forward and one 64-pr. aft, all muzzle-loading guns. In June, 1882, the *Condor* formed part of the squadron lying off Alexandria under the command of Admiral Sir Beauchamp Seymour.

On Sunday, 11th June, calling upon Captain Blomfield, the harbour-master, I found him in great distress. He had heard that there was trouble in the city, into which his wife had gone, and he was extremely anxious about her safety. We took a light carriage harnessed to a pair of Arab horses and drove into the town. Presently a great crowd came running down the street towards us. They were mostly Greeks, many of whom were wounded and bleeding.

The next moment we were surrounded by a raging mob, armed with *naboots*, or long sticks, with which they attacked us. The street was blocked from end to end; and to have attempted to drive through the mob would have been certain death. I seized the reins, swung the horses round, cleared the crowd, and drove back to the harbour-master's house. In the meantime, his wife had taken refuge in an hotel, whence she safely returned later in the day.

The officers and men of the fleet were ordered back to their ships. I went on board the flagship and reported to the admiral the condition of the town. With the trifling force at his disposal, it was impossible that he should send a landing-party ashore. Had he done so, in contravention of his orders, the handful of British seamen and Marines would have had no chance against the thousands of Egyptian soldiers who, under Arabi's instructions, were waiting in their barracks under arms, ready to turn out at the first attempt at intervention on the part of the fleet.

"WELL DONE CONDOR". THE BOMBARDMENT OF ALEXANDRIA, 1882.

During the ensuing month there poured out of Alexandria an immense number of refugees of all nations and every class of society. These were placed on board various vessels and were dispatched to the ports of their several countries. I was placed in charge of these operations; which included the chartering of ships, their preparation for passengers, and the embarkation of the refugees. In the course of the work there fell to me a task rarely included even among the infinite variety of the duties of a naval officer. My working-party was stowing native refugees in the hold of a collier, when a coloured lady was taken ill. She said: "Baby he come, sare, directly, sare, myself, sare." And so, it was. We rigged up a screen, and my coxswain and I performed the office of midwives thus thrust upon us, and all went well.

On the 10th July all merchant vessels and all foreign men-of-war left the harbour, and the British Fleet prepared for action. Admiral Seymour's squadron consisted of fifteen vessels: the ironclads *Alexandra* (flagship), Captain C. F. Hotham; *Superb*, Captain T. Le Hunte Ward; *Sultan*, Captain W. J. Hunt-Grubbe; *Téméraire*, Captain H. F. Nicholson; *Inflexible*, Captain J. A. Fisher; *Monarch*, Captain H. Fairfax, C.B.; *Invincible*, Captain R. H. M. Molyneux; *Penelope*, Captain S. J. C. D' Arcy-Irvine: the torpedo-vessel *Hecla*, Captain A. K. Wilson; gunboats *Condor*, Commander Lord C. Beresford; *Bittern*, Commander Hon. T. S. Brand; *Beacon*, Commander G. W. Hand; *Cygnet*, Lieutenant H. C. D. Ryder; *Decoy*, Lieutenant A. H. Boldero; and dispatch vessel *Helicon*, Lieutenant W. L. Morrison.

The coast fortifications extended over a front of rather more than nine miles, from Fort Marabout on the south-west to Fort Silsileh on the north-east. Midway between the two, projects the forked spit of land whose northern arm encircles the new port, and whose southern arm, extending in a breakwater, encloses the old port. The twelve forts or batteries mounted in all 261 guns and mortars.

The bombardment of Alexandria has been so thoroughly described in standard works that repetition must be unnecessary; and such interest as the present narrative may contain, must reside in the record of personal experience. I may say at once that any notoriety attached to the part borne by the *Condor* in the action was due to accidental circumstance. She happened to fight apart from the rest of the fleet and in full view of the foreign warships and merchant vessels; and, in obedience to the orders of the admiral, she had on board the correspondent of *The Times*, the late Mr. Moberly Bell. The *Condor* was actually under way when I received instructions to embark Mr. Bell. Mr. Frederic Vil-

THE BOMBARDMENT OF ALEXANDRIA, 11TH JULY, 1882

FROM CHART DRAWN BY AUTHOR AT THE TIME

liers, the artist war-correspondent, by permission of the admiral, had been my guest on board for several days. The following account of the action is taken from a private letter written at the time:—

The night before the action, I turned up all hands and made them a speech. I said that the admiral's orders were to keep out of range until an opportunity occurred. So I said to the men, 'Now, my lads, if you will rely upon me to find the opportunity, I will rely upon you to make the most of it when it occurs.' .
. . . The Marabout Fort was the second largest fort, but a long way off from the places to be attacked by the ironclads. So, the admiral had decided not to attack it at all, as he could not spare one heavy ship, and of course he would not order the small ships down there, as it was thought that they would be sunk. The orders given to the small ships were to keep out of fire, and to watch for an opportunity to occur, after the forts were silenced, to assist. *Helicon* and *Condor* were repeating ships for signals. I took station just between the two attacking fleets.

Just as the action began the *Téméraire* parted her cable and got ashore. I ran down to her and towed her off, and while doing so, saw Fort Marabout giving pepper to *Monarch*, *Invincible* and *Penelope*. Not one of these ships could be spared, as they were getting it hot and could not spare a gun for Marabout from the forts they were engaging. Seeing the difficulty, directly I had got the *Téméraire* afloat, I steamed down at full speed and engaged Fort Marabout, on the principle that according to orders 'an opportunity' had occurred. . . . I thought we should have a real rough time of it, as I knew of the heavy guns, and I knew that one shot fairly placed must sink us.

But I hoped to be able to dodge the shoals, of which there were many, and get close in, when I was quite sure they would fire over us. That is exactly what occurred. I got in close and manoeuvred the ship on the angle of the fort, so that the heavy guns could hardly bear on me, if I was very careful. The smooth-bores rained on us, but only two shots hit, the rest went short or over. One heavy shot struck the water about six feet from the ship, wetting everyone on the upper deck with spray, and bounded over us in a ricochet.

I did not fire on the smooth-bores at all until I had silenced the heavy guns which were annoying *Invincible*, *Monarch,* and

ON BOARD H.M.S. CONDOR, 11TH JULY, 1882

Penelope. The men fired splendidly. I put all down to the lectures I have given them at target practice, telling them never to throw a shot away, but always to wait until they got the sights on.

Hedworth Lambton told me afterwards that the admiral had just sent on the signal for the *Monarch* to go to Fort Marabout as soon as she could be spared, when he heard a cheer from his own men. He asked, 'What's that?' and they told him they were cheering the *Condor*. Just then our three guns were fired, and each shot hit in the middle of the heavy battery, and the *Invincible's* men burst into a cheer. The admiral said, 'Good God, she'll be sunk!' when off went our guns again, cheers rang out again from the flagship and the admiral, instead of making 'Recall *Condor*,' made 'Well done, *Condor*'. . . . at the suggestion of Hedworth Lambton, the flag-lieutenant.

We then remained there two and a half hours, and had silenced the fort all except one gun, when the signal was made to all the other small craft to assist *Condor*, and down they came and pegged away. I was not sorry, as the men were getting a bit beat. We were then recalled to the flagship, 'Captain repair on board,' and the admiral's ship's company gave us three cheers, and he himself on the quarterdeck shook me warmly by the hand, and told me he was extremely pleased. . . . I never saw such pluck as the Egyptians showed. We shelled them and shot them, but still they kept on till only one gun was left in action.

It was splendid. . . . Nothing could have been more clever than the way the admiral placed his ships. . . . The wounded are all doing well. One man had his foot shot off, and he picked it up in his hand and hopped down to the doctor with it. . . . The troops hoisted a flag of truce the day after the action; and while we waited, I sent to find out why it was they were marched away, having set fire to the town in many places. It has been burning ever since. . . .

The day after the bombardment, Captain Wilson (now Admiral of the Fleet Sir A. K. Wilson, V.C., G.C.B., O.M., G.C.V.O) hauled down the flag of the Marabout Fort and presented it to me. It is now in the Museum of the Royal Naval College, Greenwich. The commandant of Fort Marabout was so excellent an officer that when I was appointed provost-marshal and governor of the town by the admiral, I placed him on my staff to assist me in restoring order.

FORT RAS-EL-TIN AFTER BOMBARDMENT 1882

CHAPTER 3

Chief of Police

The bombardment took place on the 11th July. On the 12th, as I have narrated, the Egyptian soldiery fired the city, looted it, and evacuated the defences. On the same day the *khedive* was surrounded in his palace at Ramleh by some 400 of Arabi's cavalry and infantry, a force subsequently reduced to about 250 men. That evening Admiral Seymour was informed that the *khedive* was in danger. The admiral dispatched the *Condor* to lie off Ramleh; and there we lay all that night, rolling heavily, with a spring on the cable to enable the guns to be trained upon the sandy lane down which the soldiers must advance if they intended to take the palace.

It was arranged that, if the palace were attacked, the *khedive* should hang a white sheet from a window, and I would at once take measures to secure his safety. The night went by without alarm; and next day Tewfik, escorted by a guard of native cavalry, went to the Ras-el-Tin Palace, where he was received by Admiral Seymour and a guard of marines. Commander Hammill (who afterwards performed excellent service on the Nile), with a landing-party of 250 bluejackets and 150 marines, had already taken possession of the Ras-el-Tin Peninsula.

Upon the same day Captain John Fisher, H.M.S. *Inflexible* (afterwards Admiral of the Fleet Lord Fisher of Kilverstone, O.M.), was ordered to take command of the landing-party whose business was to secure the outer defences of the city. Captain Fisher, having occupied the lines, had a zone of anarchy, incendiarism and chaos, comprising the whole city, in the rear of his position. He at once made application for an officer to be appointed provost-marshal and chief of police, suggesting my name for the post; and the admiral gave me orders to assume this office. As a narrative written at the time owns a certain intrinsic interest, I make no apology for transcribing further passages from private letters.

. . . I landed on the 14th July, armed myself, got a horse and a guide and an escort of about thirty Egyptian cavalry, and started to overhaul the town, and see how I could best carry out my orders to 'restore law and order as soon as possible, put out fires, bury the dead, and clear the streets.' I never saw anything so awful as the town on that Friday; streets, square, and blocks of buildings all on fire, roaring and crackling and tumbling about like a hell let loose, Arabs murdering each other for loot under my nose, wretches running about with fire-balls and torches to light up new places, all the main thoroughfares impassable from burning fallen houses, streets with many corpses in them, mostly murdered by the Arab soldiers for loot—these corpses were Arabs murdered by each other—in fact, a pandemonium of hell and its devils.

I took a chart with me and arranged the different parts of the town where I should make depots and police stations. The admiral could only spare me 60 bluejackets and 70 marines from the British Fleet; but he obtained a proportionate number from the foreign warships. By sunset I had 620 men in the different depots, mostly foreigners. . . . I had only 140 men to patrol the town, to stop the looting, to stop the 'fresh burning' of houses, to bury the corpses, and to protect the lives of those who had come on shore. By quickly sending the men about in parties in different parts of the town, and by employing Arabs to inform me when and where certain houses might be burnt, I often managed to get a patrol there just in time to stop it, and the people thought there were 600 police in the town instead of 140.

For the foreign bluejackets were ordered to occupy their respective legations and not to take any part in restoring order. This was of course in the first seventy-two hours, during which time neither myself nor my men slept one wink, as at 12 o'clock on two occasions an alarm was sounded that Arabi was attacking the lines, and all of us had to peg away to the front, where we had to remain until daylight, expecting attack every moment. These alarms lost many houses, as the mob set them alight while we were at the front; however, it was unavoidable. On Monday, 17th July, I was sent 400 more men (bluejackets) in answer to my urgent appeal to the admiral, as so many fanatic Arabs were coming into the town, . . . but on Tuesday the 18th the bluejackets were all ordered off to their ships and 600 picked marines were sent in their place. . . . After I had planned to get the town into order on the Friday (14th) I went to the arsenal and wrote a proclamation. . . .

I went off to the admiral on the following (Saturday) morning, and submitted that I should be allowed to post the proclamation throughout the town. Sir A. Colvin and the *khedive* were strongly opposed to the proclamation; but the admiral approved of the scheme. Some of the authorities suggested that if I shot anybody it would be well to shoot him at night, or in the prisons, and then no one would know, and there would be no row. This I stoutly refused, demanding my own way for restoring order, and saying that a fair honest proclamation was the proper line to take, as all persons would then know what would happen to them if they committed certain specified acts. I carried my point, and the admiral supported me, and on Saturday night (15th) I had the whole town proclaimed in Arabic, stating that persons caught firing houses would be shot, persons caught looting twice would be shot; all persons to return to their homes, etc., with confidence, and anyone wanting to get information or to lodge complaints to repair instantly to the chief of police.

By Wednesday (19th) I had perfect order in the town, and all firing of houses had been stopped, life was comparatively safe, looting nearly stopped. By Friday the 21st, one week after taking charge, all the fires were put out, all the corpses buried, and things were generally ship-shape. I could not have done this unless the admiral had trusted entirely to me, and given me absolute power of life and death, or to flog, or to blow down houses, or to do anything that I thought fit to restore law and order and to put the fires out. I only had to shoot five men by drumhead court-martial sentence, besides flogging a certain number, to effect what I have told you.

I had a clear thoroughfare through every street in the town by Monday (24th), and all debris from fallen houses piled up each side and all dangerous walls pulled down. These things were done by organising large working parties of from 100 to 200 hired Arabs. At first, I collected them at the point of the bayonet

At corner of the Rue des Sœurs, Alexandria.
14th July 1882.

Provost-Marshal Beauchamp
"marshalling the Town"

PROVOST-MARSHAL AND CHIEF OF POLICE. ALEXANDRIA,
JULY, 1882

and made them work, but I paid them a good wage every evening, and the bayonets were unnecessary after the first day, when they found that England would pay well.

I also collected all the fire-engines I could find, bought some, and requisitioned others, got some artificers from the Fleet and got the engines in order, had a bluejacket fire-brigade, and also a working party of Arabs on the same footing as the road brigade. These worked exclusively at the fires, and not at patrolling unless at urgent necessity. Besides these I had a sanitary committee, which buried any bodies we might have missed, burned refuse and remains of loot about the streets, and reburied any bodies which might not have been buried deep enough, besides enforcing cleanliness directly the town began to get a little bit shipshape. There was a corps of native police to work under my patrols, and when I turned all the affairs over, I had 260 of these men.

I disarmed all Europeans found in the streets with revolvers, and by so doing saved many a row in the town, as the class I have mentioned returned in thousands after the bombardment, and they treated the Arabs as if they, the Europeans, had silenced the forts and policed the town. I put many in irons for looting, and for shooting at inoffensive Arabs.

The greatest triumph was the formation of an Egyptian court to try the serious cases I had on hand for life and death and long terms of imprisonment. Not only did I get the court formed to try what cases I chose to bring before it, but after sentence of death I insisted on Egyptian authorities making the Egyptian soldiers (the loyal ones) themselves shooting the prisoners whom the court sentenced. . . .

I had four gallopers and four marine orderly gallopers, in default of whom I could not have done things so quickly in the many different departments, nineteen horses, and a telephone to each station. I paid all the carts requisitioned in the town for carrying my men's provisions, loot, etc. etc. The officer using them signed a chit stating the hour he had taken a cart and for what service, and then the man came to my office to be paid, which he was instantly. By this means good feeling was established between the people and the military police. Each depot had two interpreters attached to it to avoid any misunderstanding, and for explanations when trying prisoners and interrogating witnesses. . . .

The marine officer thoroughly investigated each case, examined all witnesses, and then placed the evidence on a regular charge-sheet, stating whether he believed the prisoner guilty or not guilty, and his reason for that opinion. If it was a serious case, I again tried it myself and judged accordingly. There were several cases of blackmailing at first, but these were soon stopped. . . .

Besides the courts held at the Police Depots, courts were held at the Tribunal Zaptieh and the Caracol l'A'ban, at which Egyptian officers acted as judges. In each court were three shorthand-writers, each placed behind a separate screen, and under the charge of a sergeant of marines, to prevent collusion, who submitted their reports to me, in order that I should receive three independent accounts of the proceedings, upon which I could intervene, if necessary, in order to prevent anyone being shot if there were not the clearest and most uncompromising evidence of his guilt. If there were any discrepancy in the reports, I had the prisoner retried. I did this in three cases. Another case, in which the circumstantial evidence, though very strong, was not conclusive, I reprieved.

The following troops assisted the British forces in restoring order: 125 Americans, about the American Consulate; 30 Germans, about the German Consulate and Hospital; and 140 Greeks about the Greek Consulate and Hospital. On the 16th July, Captain Briscoe (a son of an old Waterford man who hunted the Curraghmore hounds after the death of my uncle, Henry Lord Waterford) of the P. and O. *Tanjore* volunteered his services, and with 20 Italians of his crew, did excellent work. Other volunteers who assisted me were Mr. Towrest, a member of the Customs, and Mr. Wallace. Major Hemel, R.M.L.I., and Captain Creaghi, R.M.L.I., were appointed magistrates. These marine officers performed invaluable services.

I had special reason to be grateful to Mr. John Ross, a British merchant of Alexandria, who gave me every assistance in his power. He knew every yard of the place. He gave me invaluable advice with regard to the organisation of the city, obtained interpreters, and helped to supply the troops, placing his stores at my disposal. He would have dispensed with receipts for articles supplied, had I not insisted upon his taking them. Mr. Ross supplied the whole Fleet with coal, fresh meat, and all necessaries; his help was quite inestimable, his energy and patriotism beyond praise; but although he must have suffered considerable losses, he received no recognition of any kind from the Government except the naval medal.

Mr. Ross gave me great assistance also in parcelling out Mehemet Ali Square among the country purveyors of produce, each of whom received a permit, written in English and in Arabic, to occupy a certain space, duly pegged out, in which to put up their booths. This measure restored confidence. One old lady, a stout person of Levantine origin, thought that the permit entitled her to perpetual freehold; and she subsequently attempted to sue the Egyptian Government for damages, producing my permit as evidence.

Upon first going ashore to restore order, I found whole streets blocked with smouldering ruins. Putting my horse at one such obstacle, I scrambled over it; and I had scarce reached the other side when a wall fell bodily behind me, cutting off my escort, who had to fetch a compass round the side streets to rejoin me.

Without taking the smallest notice of me or of my escort, men were shooting at one another, quarrelling over loot, and staggering along, laden with great bundles, like walking balloons. The streets were speedily cleared of these rioters by the use of machine guns. The method adopted was to fire the gun over their heads, and as they fled, to run the gun round turnings and head them off again, so that they received the impression that the town was full of guns. On no occasion did I fire the gun at them. The principles upon which order was restored were to punish disobedience, to enlist labour and to pay for it fairly.

The prisoners taken were organised in separate gangs, set to work, and paid less than the rest of the labourers. The most critical part of the business of extinguishing fires and preventing incendiarism occurred at the Tribunal, which was stored with property worth many thousands of pounds. A fire-engine was purchased for its protection at a cost of £160, 18s. 1d. The total expenses of the restoration or order were, I think, under £2,000. During the fortnight I was on shore, every station and port was visited at least once a day and twice a night.

On one such inspection I gave my horse to an Arab lad to hold. A few minutes afterwards there was the crack of a pistol. I ran out, and there was the boy lying on the ground, a bullet-wound in his chest. To satisfy his curiosity he had been fingering the 4-barrel Lancaster pistol in the holster, and that was the end of *him*, poor lad.

Upon another occasion, when I was at work in one of my stations, a sudden tumult arose in the street. I went out, to perceive a huge Irish marine artilleryman engaged in furious conflict with five or six men of the patrol. They had got handcuffs on him, and he was fighting with manacled hands. I asked the sergeant what was the matter.

"He's drunk, sir. We are going to lock him up."

"Let him go," I said.

The men fell back; and the Irishman, seeing an iron railing, raised his hands above his head and brought them down upon the iron, smashing the handcuffs, and turned upon me like a wild beast at bay. The man was in a frenzy. Standing directly in front of him, I spoke to him quietly.

"Now, my lad, listen to me. You' re an Irishman." He looked down at me. "You' re an Irishman, and you've had a little too much to drink, like many of us at times. But you are all right. Think a moment. Irishmen don't behave like this in the presence of the enemy. Nor will you. Why, we may be in a tight place tomorrow, and who's going to back me then? You are. You're worth fifty of the enemy. You're the man I want."

As I talked to him, the expression of his face changed from desperation to a look of bewilderment, and from bewilderment to understanding; and then he suddenly broke down. He turned his head aside and cried. I told the sergeant to take him away and give him some tea.

Having heard from the Governor of Alexandria that a quantity of arms was concealed in a village lying a few miles outside the city, I took thither a party of Egyptian military police and a guard of Marines. On the way we were joined by some 800 British soldiers, who surrounded the village, while the police conducted a house-to-house search. A certain newspaper correspondent accompanied me. The police knocked at the door of a house, and received no reply; whereupon the correspondent drew his revolver and incontinently blew in the lock. I told him that he had no right to do such a thing; that he might have killed innocent persons; and that he must not do it again.

"Oh, but," says he, "you don't understand how to do these things."

I requested him to understand that I was provost-marshal, and that unless he obeyed orders, he would be sent back to Alexandria.

"Oh, but," says he, "you can't do that. You don't understand—"

"Sergeant!" said I, "a file of marines."

"Oh, but," protested the correspondent, "you can't—"

"Sergeant, take this gentleman back to Alexandria."

It was a long walk and a hot walk home.

On the 17th July, General Sir Archibald Alison took command of the land forces. At the request of the general, the admiral ordered me to remain in command of the police until 1st August, when I was relieved by Major Gordon. It was about this time that Captain Fisher devised his armoured train, which, carrying armed bluejackets, made daily sorties. A bluejacket sitting on the rail was ordered to come down by his officer.

"I can't see 'em from down below," he said. The next moment he was hit by a bullet. "They've found the range, sir," said he, as he tumbled over.

Admiral Sir Beauchamp Seymour was good enough to address to me a very gratifying letter of commendation for my services. Among the many kind congratulations I received, I valued especially the letters from the captains under whom I had served in various ships, and many admirals with whom I had served. On 11th July I was promoted to the rank of captain. In the following September the Admiralty forwarded to Admiral Sir Beauchamp Seymour (raised in November to a peerage as Baron Alcester) the expression of their satisfaction at the services of Captain Fisher and of myself.

I overheard a lady finding great fault with my old chief, Sir Beauchamp Seymour. I asked her what she had against Lord Alcester.

"Why," said she, "he is a Goth and a Vandal. Did he not burn the Alexandrian Library?"

A sequel to the work in Alexandria was my conversation with Mr. Gladstone on the subject, which took place upon my return home some weeks later. Mr. Gladstone sent for me; and after most courteously expressing his appreciation of my services, he discussed the question of compensation to the inhabitants of Alexandria who had suffered loss and damage. The information he required I had carefully collected in Alexandria by means of an organised intelligence corps, upon each of whom was impressed the fact that if he gave false information he would most certainly be punished.

My view was then, and is now, that the whole of the claims might have been justly settled for a million sterling, upon these conditions: that the question should be tackled at once; that all palpably unwarranted claims should be repudiated from the outset, because if they were recorded as claims there would eventually be no way of rebutting them, and it would be found necessary to pay them ultimately; that doubtful claims should be held over for consideration; and that the proved claims should be paid immediately. The important point was that in order to avoid difficulties in disputes in the future, the matter should be dealt with at once.

I knew of a case (and of other similar cases) in which a jeweller who had contrived to remove the whole of his stock into safety after the riot, put in a claim for the value of the whole of the said goods.

These considerations I laid before Mr. Gladstone, informing him also, in the light of the special information which had come to my knowledge, that if the matter were allowed to drift, the sum to be disbursed, instead of being about a million, would probably amount to some four millions.

In the event, the International Commission of Indemnities paid £4,341,011.

CHAPTER 4

Garrison Work

When I was relieved, on 1st August (1882), of the post of provost-marshal and chief of police, the *Condor* was ordered to keep the Mex lines and citadel, which defended the south-western boundary of Alexandria, forming a barrier across the long and narrow strip of land which extends between the sea and Lake Mareotis, and upon which the city is built. The fortifications of the sea front were continued, with a brief interval, at right angles to the sea face, extending no more than some three-quarters of the distance across the strip of land, so that between one end of the fortifications and the sea, and between the other end and the shore of Lake Mareotis, there were undefended spaces.

It was therefore necessary to frame a plan of defence with the force and materials at command, sufficient to hold this left flank of the city against the large bodies of rebel soldiery and Arabs hovering in the vicinity. Thirty men from the *Condor* were brought on shore, with the band, which, consisting of one drum and one fife, was few and humble but convincing.

The two forts on the earthwork were manned; a 40-pounder smooth-bore taken from one of the Mex Forts was mounted on the roof of the fort nearest to Lake Mareotis, whence it was fired at regular intervals at the enemy occupying the earthworks on the farther shore of the lake. After five days they were knocked out of the place. Charges were made for the gun out of the miscellaneous ammunition found in the Mex Forts.

The gun used to capsize almost every time it was fired. It was served by a Maltese gunner, who became so superstitiously devoted to his commanding officer, that when I was relieved by Colonel Earle, my Maltese never received an order without observing that "Lord Charles Beresford not do that, sare"; until Earle lost patience, as well he might.

"D—n Lord Charles Beresford!" said he.

Wire entanglements were fixed along the face of the earthworks. In the two open spaces at the ends of the line of fortifications, rockets were buried, and a lanyard was led along from the firing tube to a peg in the ground, so that anyone passing that way at night would trip over the lanyard, thus firing the rocket, and causing a beautiful fountain of fire to spring from the ground, lighting up the whole locality. The device soon stopped nocturnal intrusions.

The open space at the Mareotis end was also commanded by a Gatling gun mounted on the roof of the fort. In the forts and earthworks were about twenty miscellaneous guns. These were all kept loaded; the powder being taken from the vast amount of loose powder stored in the Mex lines. The guns were connected with trigger lines to the forts, so that the whole lot could be fired from one place. The railway lines leading from Mex Harbour through the fortification, and, on the other side of the strip of land, from the causeway leading across Lake Mareotis into the city, were repaired.

The railway bridge by Lake Mareotis was repaired, and a torpedo was placed beneath it in case of attack. A picquet of Marines occupied a truck placed on the bridge. The train was set running. The two drawbridges leading to the forts were repaired. The men garrisoning the works were housed in tents made out of the sails of the Arab dhows lying in Mex camber. A tank was obtained from Alexandria, and fresh water brought into it. On the sea side of the position, the *Condor* commanded the flank of the approaches.

Having thus secured this flank of the city against attack, so that it could be held against a large force, it was necessary to make reconnaissances into the surrounding country. The little landing-party went ashore every evening at 5.30 (with the band, few and humble but convincing) and occupied the lines. Every morning at seven o'clock they returned to the ship; and during the afternoon went out upon reconnaissance, accompanied by a boat's gun mounted in a bullock cart, and a rocket-tube mounted on another bullock cart.

Two horses were harnessed to each cart, assisted, when required, by bluejackets hauling on drag-ropes. The men of the *Condor* were reinforced from the Fleet on these expeditions, so that the total force of bluejackets and marines was 150. The cavalry being represented solely by the colonel and the major of marines, and myself, who were mounted, we had no sufficient force wherewith to pursue the flying foe.

We used to play hide-and-seek with the soldiery and Bedouin

GATLING GUN AND CREW

A GATLING GUN

among the sandhills. When they approached on one flank, we shelled them with the little gun until they retired; and then, hauling the gun-cart and rocket-cart over the roughest ground, we suddenly appeared and shelled them on the other flank, to their great amazement. All hands enjoyed these expeditions amazingly.

In the course of these reconnaissances, large quantities of stores and ammunition were found in the neighbouring villages. About three miles from the lines, an immense store of gun-cotton and Abel's detonators was discovered in a quarry among the low hills, stored in a shed. As no hostile force appeared during the next two days, I determined to destroy the gun-cotton. Captain A. K. Wilson of the *Hecla* sent 20 bluejackets and six marines to assist me. These were embarked and landed within half a mile of the place. Outposts were set, with orders to signal should the enemy appear, and the rest of the party set to work.

Although gun-cotton does not, strictly speaking, explode except by detonation, it is extremely difficult to define where ignition ends and detonation begins; and there had been instances of its explosion, supposed to be due to the internal pressure of a large mass. A tremendous explosion of gun-cotton had occurred in 1866 at Stowmarket, where its manufacture was being carried on under the patent of Sir Frederick Abel, then chemist to the War Office. On another occasion, when Sir Frederick was conducting an experiment designed to prove that ignition was harmless, he had his clothes blown off his body, and narrowly escaped with his life.

Recollecting these things, I thought it advisable to spread the stuff in a loose mass upon the hillside sloping to the quarry. The gun-cotton was packed in boxes. These were unpacked, and the contents were spread on the ground. Next to the pile, a bucket of loose powder was poured on the ground and over the fuse, to make sure of ignition. Into the powder was led one end of a Bickford's fuse, which was then threaded through the discs of gun-cotton. The fuse was timed to burn for five minutes.

The work was highly exhausting to the men, and more than once I felt inclined to call in the outposts to help; but I decided that it would not be right to take the risk of a surprise attack; for we were working in a trap, being closed in by the quarries on one side and by the low hills on the other. And sure enough, when the men had been working for five hours, up went the outpost's signal, and the corporal of marines with his three men came running in to report that large numbers of the enemy were in sight.

Hastening out, I saw about 50 scouts running up, an action so unusual that it was evident they were strongly supported. Presently, about 200 skirmishers appeared, and behind them a large body of cavalry, probably about 700 in number. The outposts were at once recalled. The men were ordered out of the quarry, divided into two companies of twelve men each, and retired by companies over the hill towards the shore, out of sight of the enemy. Mr. Attwood, the gunner of the *Hecla*, a bluejacket and myself, remained to fire the fuse. It was a five-minute fuse. The retreating men had been told to count as they ran, and at the end of four minutes, or when they saw us lie down, to halt and lie down. I gave the order in case there should be an explosion. When the men were lying down, I fired the fuse. Then the gunner, the bluejacket and I ran about 300 yards, and flung ourselves down.

Then there came a noise as though a giant had expelled a huge breath; the blast of the ignition burned our cheeks; in the midst of a vast column of yellow smoke, boxes and pieces of paper were whirling high in air, and a strong wind sucked back into the vacuum, almost dragging us along the sand. The enemy were so interested in the spectacle that they gave us time to get back to the boats.

It is probable that information had been given to the hostile forces by the inhabitants of the village past which we went to reach the quarry where was the gun-cotton; for, in retreating to the boats, when I looked back, instead of the 20 or 30 native women who were usually sitting about the place, I saw about 200 men eagerly watching us from the house-tops, evidently in the hope of enjoying the gratifying spectacle of our destruction.

From the summit of the slope falling to the sea, I signalled to the flagship, with a handkerchief tied to a pole, that I was surrounded: one of the many occasions upon which a knowledge of signalling proved invaluable. There was a haze upon the water, and I could not clearly discern the answering signal; but the signalman of the flagship had seen my figure silhouetted on the sky-line. Instantly after, Captain John Fisher of the *Inflexible* manned and armed boats, came ashore, and the enemy immediately retreated.

Shortly afterwards, as I was now a captain, I was relieved of the command of the *Condor* by Commander Jeffreys, and went on half-pay. I should naturally have much preferred to remain in my little ship; but she was not a captain's command; and I left her (as I see I wrote at the time) with a tear in each eye. Commander Jeffreys discovered the place where she had been hit during the bombardment, one of her underwater plates having been started. Until then, it was thought that the only damage consisted of a hole through her awning and the smashing of a boat.

At the conclusion of this period of my service, I was most gratified to receive a gracious message of congratulation from Her Majesty the Queen.

H.H. the *Khedive* wrote to me, kindly expressing his sense of my services, and at the same time offering me an appointment upon his staff, in which capacity I was to go to the front. Lord Granville and the Admiralty having signified their permission that I should accept the post, I left Alexandria for Ismailia, together with several members of the *khedival* staff.

We went by steamer, which towed a huge iron lighter carrying horses. A beam ran from stem to stern of the lighter, and to it the horses were tethered with halters. I remarked to the captain of the steamer that it would be advisable, in order to avoid injuring the lighter, to take every precaution to prevent the steamer from having to go astern. But in Ismailia Bay, which was crowded with shipping, a vessel crossed the steamer's bows, the steamer was forced to go astern, and she cut a hole in the lighter with her propeller.

One of the ship's officers instantly descended the Jacob's ladder into the lighter with me, and we cut the halters of the horses, just in time to free them before the lighter sank, and there we were swimming about among the wild and frightened stallions. By splashing the water into their faces, we turned one or two shorewards, when the rest followed and came safely to land.

Upon discussing the matter of my appointment to the staff of the *khedive* with Sir Garnet Wolseley, to my surprise he declined to permit me to accept it. Discipline is discipline, and there was nothing for it but to acquiesce.

I was about packing up my things, when Mr. Cameron, the war correspondent of *The Standard*, informed me that he was authorised to appoint a correspondent to *The New York Herald*, and also that he had permission to send the said correspondent to the front, where I particularly desired to go. The notion attracted me. I applied to the military authorities for permission to accept the offer. Permission was, however, refused. So, there was nothing to do but to go home. But before starting, I consoled myself by sending some provisions, privately, to the unfortunate officers at the front, who, owing to the substitution

British troop train with Nordenfelt gun in Egypt 1882

by the transport people of tents for food, were short of necessaries.

I obtained from the *Orient* four large boxes filled with potted lobster, salmon, sardines, beef, tins of cocoa, and so forth, and sent one box each to the 1st Life Guards, the Blues, the Guards, and the Royal Marines. The orders were that no private supplies were to go up. These I ventured to disregard; got up bright and early at three o'clock in the morning; and had the boxes stowed under the hay which was being sent up in railway trucks, before officialdom was out of bed. Then I went home.

I consider that Sir Garnet Wolseley's conduct of the campaign, and his brilliant victory at Tel-el-Kebir, were military achievements of a high order. The public, perhaps, incline to estimate the merit of an action with reference to the loss of life incurred, rather than in relation to the skill employed in attaining the object in view. The attack at dawn at Tel-el-Kebir was a daring conception brilliantly carried into execution. Many persons, both at the time and subsequently, have explained how it ought to have been done. But Sir Garnet Wolseley did it.

The public seem to appreciate a big butcher's bill, although it may be caused by stupidity or by lack of foresight on the part of the general. But if he retrieves his mistakes, the public think more of him than of the general who, by the exercise of foresight and knowledge, wins an action with little loss of life.

I carried home with me a 64 lb. shell fired from the *Condor* at the Mex magazine, intending to present it to the Prince of Wales. I found it in the sand. It had passed right through the walls of the magazine, and it had not exploded. Having brought it on board the *Condor*, I caused the gunner, Mr. Alexander Greening, to sound it with a copper rod; and he came to the conclusion that it was empty of gunpowder. I therefore thought that it had never been filled. I intended to have it cut in two and a lamp for the prince made of the pieces, and took it to Nordenfelt's works for the purpose.

The foreman, desirous of taking every precaution before cutting it, had it again filled with water and sounded with a copper rod, when it suddenly exploded, blowing off the foot of the workman who held it, and doing other serious damage. The explanation seems to be that the force of the impact when the shell was fired had solidified the powder into a hard mass. But explanation would have little availed had the shell burst in the smoking-room at Sandringham, where a fragment of it remains to this day.

CHAPTER 5

Passing Through Egypt

At the beginning of the year 1883 I was on my way out to India with Lady Charles in the P. and O. s.s. *Malwa*. Proceeding into Ismailia Lake, the *Malwa* was rammed by another vessel which tried to cross the *Malwa's* bows. I was looking over the side of the *Malwa* and I saw a curious thing. I saw the colliding vessel rebound from the *Malwa* and strike her again. I ran up to the bridge, where the captain had already given orders to stop the engines. The ship was sinking; it was no time to stand upon ceremony; and I ventured to suggest to the captain that he should put his engines full steam ahead, when he might hope to beach the vessel, whereas if she stayed where she was, she would infallibly go down in deep water. The captain, like a good seaman, gave the order, and the chief engineer carried it into execution with admirable promptitude. I went down into the engine-room and found the water already rising through the foot-plates.

As the ship steamed towards the shore, settling down as she went, I stood with Lady Charles on the bridge, telling her that, if the vessel sank, I should throw her overboard—although she could not swim—and should jump in after her. To which she merely replied, "That will be very disagreeable!"

The ship was safely beached, though not before the water had risen to my cabin. She was afterwards salved by the help of the Navy. H.M.S. *Carysfort*, commanded by Captain H. F. Stephenson, C.B. (now Admiral Sir Henry F. Stephenson, G.C.V.O., K.C.B., Gentleman Usher of the Black Rod), sent a carpenter and a working party; and they did excellent service in the *Malwa*.

Our party went to Cairo, there to await the next steamer.

Hicks Pasha and his staff dined with us upon the night before they left Cairo, upon their fatal expedition. Colonel W. Hicks had been appointed by the *khedive* chief of the staff of the Army of the Soudan. In the following August he was appointed commander-in-chief. From

Cairo he went to Souakim, thence to Berber, and thence to Khartoum. On the 28th April, he fought a successful action on the White Nile, south of Khartoum, in which his Egyptian troops did well. In September, Hicks left Duem with his staff and some 10,000 men and marched into the desert, which swallowed them up. The whole army was exterminated by the *Mahdi's dervishes*. Gordon said that the *Mahdi* built with the skulls of the slain a pyramid.

I applied for permission to accompany Hicks Pasha, but my old friend Lord Dufferin was determined that I should not go upon that hazardous enterprise. I believe he telegraphed to the Government on the subject. At any rate, he had his way, and so saved my life.

In October, before the news of the disaster had reached Cairo, the British Army of Occupation had been reduced from 6,700 men to 3,000. Subsequently, the British Government proceeded with the policy of abandoning the Soudan, in one phase of which I was to bear my part.

In the meantime, Lady Charles and I joined the Duke of Portland and his party, among whom were Lord de Grey and Lord Wenlock; went to India; enjoyed some excellent sport; and returned home.

CHAPTER 6

The Soudan War of 1884-5

SUMMARY OF EVENTS

A year before the British forces restored order in Egypt, trouble was beginning in the Soudan. One Mahomet Ahmed, who was the son of a boat-builder, and who had the peculiar conformation of the teeth which betokened the fore-ordained of the Prophet, announced that he was the *Mahdi*. In July, 1881, the holy man dwelt upon the island of Abba, on the White Nile, above Khartoum. Thence he caused it to be made known that he was the chosen instrument for the reformation of Islam, and that all those who denied him would be abolished. Reouf Pasha, who was then Governor-General of the Soudan, summoned the *Mahdi* to Khartoum, there to give an account of himself. The *Mahdi* naturally refused; and when Reouf sent soldiers to fetch him, the *Mahdi* slew most of them, and departed into the hills, he and all his following.

The Governor of Fashoda took an expedition to Gheddeer, and was also slain, together with most of his men. Then Giegler Pasha, a German, acting as temporary Governor-General of the Soudan, succeeded in defeating the forces of the *Mahdi*. But Abdel Kader, who, succeeding Reouf, took over the command from Giegler, was defeated in his turn. On 7th June, 1882, the Egyptian forces were cut to pieces near Fashoda. In July, the *Mahdi* was besieging Obeid and Bara. By October, 1882, both places were in danger of falling, and Abdel Kader was demanding reinforcements from Egypt.

The Soudan is a country as large as India; at that time, it had no railways, no canals, no roads, and, excepting the Nile during a part of the year, no navigable rivers. In November, 1882, the British Government informed the *khedive* that they declined to be responsible for the condition of the Soudan. Lord Granville's intimation to this effect was the first step in the policy which progressed from blunder to blunder to the desertion and death of General Gordon.

The Egyptian Government, left in the lurch, hastily enlisted some 10,000 men, the most part being brought in by force, and dispatched them to Abdel Kader at Berber. At Abdel Kader's request, Colonel Stewart and two other British officers were sent to Khartoum to help him to deal with the raw and mutinous levies.

In December, a number of British officers were appointed to the Egyptian Army in Egypt, in accordance with the recommendations of Lord Dufferin, and Sir Evelyn Wood was appointed *Sirdar*. The British Army of Occupation had now been reduced to 12,000 men, under the command of General Sir Archibald Alison, who, in the following April (1883) was succeeded by Lieutenant-General F. C. S. Stephenson.

In January, 1883, Colonel W. Hicks, afterwards Hicks Pasha, was appointed by the *khedive* chief of the staff of the Army of the Soudan. Before he proceeded to the theatre of war, Abdel Kader had lost and won various engagements, and had reoccupied the province of Sennar; while the *Mahdi* had taken El Obeid and Bara and occupied the whole of Kordofan.

In February, it was announced in the Queen's Speech that "the British troops will be withdrawn as promptly as may be permitted by a prudent examination of the country"; a declaration provoking intense alarm among the European inhabitants of Egypt. Their protests, however, were totally disregarded. The Egyptians naturally concluded that England owned no real interest in that reform of administration which her influence alone could achieve.

On 7th February, 1883, Colonel Hicks left Cairo for Khartoum, with his staff, consisting of Colonels Colborne and De Cöetlogon, Majors Farquhar and Martin, and Captains Warner, Massey and Forrestier-Walker. Upon the night before their departure, Colonel Hicks and his staff dined with Lord and Lady Charles Beresford in Cairo. Lord Charles Beresford, who was then on half-pay, had expressed a wish to accompany Colonel Hicks, but Lord Dufferin disapproving of his suggestion, Lord Charles Beresford withdrew it.

Hicks and his men disappeared into the desert, which presently swallowed them up.

On the 28th April, Hicks defeated a large force of the *Mahdi*'s army on the White Nile. The Egyptian Government then decided to reconquer the province of Kordofan, and dispatched reinforcements to Khartoum. On the 9th September, Hicks Pasha, at the head of

10,000 men, marched for Duem. The last dispatch received from him was dated 3rd October, 1883. Upon a day early in November, Hicks and his whole army were annihilated.

His defeat left Khartoum in great danger. On 9th November, before the news of the disaster reached England, the British Government stated that all British troops were to be withdrawn from Egypt. When the fact was known, the decision of the government was modified; but they still declined to interfere in the Soudan; and advised the Egyptian Government to evacuate at least a part of that territory. The Egyptian Government protesting, the British Government, on 4th January, 1884, sent a peremptory message insisting that the policy of evacuation should be carried into execution. The inconsequence of Her Majesty's Ministers is sufficiently apparent.

In the meantime, during August of the preceding year, 1883, trouble had arisen in the Eastern Soudan, where Osman Digna, a trader, joined the *Mahdi*, and brought all the tribes of that country to his standard. At the beginning of November, 1883, just at the time when Hicks Pasha and his army had come to their end, an Egyptian force under Mahmoud Talma Pasha was defeated by Osman Digna in the attempt to relieve Tokar, besieged by the rebels, Captain Moncrieff, Royal Navy, British Consul at Souakim, being killed in the action. A second expeditionary force under Suleiman Pasha was cut to pieces on 2nd December at Tamanieh.

The Egyptian Government then dispatched reinforcements under the command of General Valentine Baker, among whose staff were Colonel Sartorius, Lieutenant-Colonel Harrington, Lieutenant-Colonel Hay, Majors Harvey, Giles, and Holroyd, Morice Bey and Dr. Leslie. On the 4th February, 1884, Baker was defeated at El-Teb, with the loss of nearly two-thirds of his force. Morice Bey, Dr. Leslie, and nine other European officers were killed. Souakim being threatened, Admiral Hewett, on 10th December, was given the command of the town, having under him some 3,800 troops.

Two days later came the news of the taking of Sinkat by the rebels, and of the massacre of the garrison. During the period in which these successive disasters occurred, the British Army of Occupation was kept idle in Cairo by the orders of the British Government.

The current of events now divides, one leading to Khartoum, the other still flowing in the Eastern Soudan. The British Government, hopelessly at fault, turned to General Charles Gordon, as the one man in the world who could apparently perform miracles. Ten years previously, "Chinese" Gordon, as Governor-General of the Soudan, and again in 1877, as Governor-General of the Soudan, Darfur and the Equatorial Provinces, had freed the country from Turkish rule, broken the slave trade, established peace, opened trade routes, and laid the foundations of civilisation. Since 1877 he had been engaged in setting wrong things right in Egypt in the Soudan again, in Abyssinia, in China, in the Mauritius, at the Cape, in Palestine, and in the Congo.

On 18th January, 1884, Gordon was instructed by the British Government to report upon the best method of evacuating the Soudan. When he arrived at Cairo, these instructions were radically altered by Sir Evelyn Baring (afterwards Lord Cromer), who, on the 25th January, informed Gordon that he was required actually to direct the evacuation of Khartoum and of the whole Soudan, and afterwards to establish an organised government in that country. Gordon arrived at Khartoum on the 18th February, where he was hailed as the father and saviour of the people. (*Vide Gordon* by Demetrius Charles Boulger: Leonaur 2009.)

On the same day, Major-General Sir Gerald Graham left Suez to join at Souakim the force which had been placed under his command. That force was chiefly drawn from the British Army of Occupation in Egypt. The object of the expedition was the relief of Tokar, or, if that place had already fallen, the protection of Souakim, an alternative which involved an attack upon Osman Digna's victorious army. Tokar was in fact taken by the enemy before the expedition started.

The British Government, whose original intention had been to refrain from any action in the Soudan whatsoever; which had been compelled by force of circumstances, including the most frightful bloodshed, to change a wholly negative policy to a definite scheme of evacuation; now perceived, of course too late, that if the European population was to be brought away, at least some measure of military force must be employed. What Her Majesty's Ministers were unable to see, or what, if they saw, they chose to ignore, was the plain fact that the same force and the same measures and the same promptitude would be required for the salvation of Europeans in face of the enemy, as for the reconquest and reoccupation of the country. In this delusion, or dereliction, resides the explanation of an affair which has left an indelible stain upon British honour.

On 28th February, 1884, Graham defeated the enemy, inflicting upon them severe losses, at El-Teb, near the spot upon which Baker's disastrous action had occurred some three weeks previously. On 13th

March, after a hard and at times a dubious fight, Graham won another victory at Tamai, and the power of Osman Digna was broken. Graham was then ordered to return, and the expedition was over.

By withdrawing Graham's troops, the Government both threw away the fruits of his success, and deliberately abandoned the control of the Souakim-Berber route from Khartoum, by which alone Gordon could have brought away the refugees. Berber was the key to the Soudan. Thenceforth, the Souakim-Berber route was impracticable; and it was for this reason that Lord Wolseley was obliged to take the much longer Nile route.

On the very day after Graham's victory at El-Teb, and before Graham had left Souakim, Gordon had telegraphed from Khartoum as follows:—

> There is not much chance of the situation improving, and every chance of it getting worse; for we have nothing to rely on to make it better. You must, therefore, decide whether you will or will not make an attempt to save the two-thirds of the population who are well affected before these two-thirds retreat. Should you wish to intervene, send 200 British troops to Wady Haifa, and adjutants to inspect Dongola, and then open up Souakim-Berber road by Indian Moslem troops. This will cause an immediate collapse of the revolt.

On 2nd March he telegraphed again to the same effect; but Lord Granville declined to accede to General Gordon's suggestions. A few days later, when the Eastern Soudan and the Souakim-Berber route had been definitely abandoned, Sir Evelyn Baring strongly advised the British Government to obtain command of the Souakim-Berber route. But the advice was refused by Lord Granville, and the most urgent appeals continued to be addressed to him in vain.

Deserted by the government, Gordon tried, and failed, to raise money privately for the purpose of engaging Turkish troops. Early in April, Khartoum was closely besieged. At this time, Lord Wolseley urged upon the Government the necessity of relieving Gordon. In May, preparations for war were begun. A part of the British Army of Occupation in Egypt was sent up the Nile; and Commander Hammill and other naval officers were employed to report upon the navigation of the river.

These facts did not prevent Lord Hartington from informing the House of Commons, early in July, that the Government had no intention of sending an expedition to relieve General Gordon, unless it were made clear that by no other means could he be relieved, and adding that the Government had "received no information making it desirable that we should depart from that decision" (Royle, *The Egyptian Campaigns*: Leonaur 2013). On 24th July, Lord Wolseley made a spirited protest against the procrastination of the Government. The pressure of public opinion could no longer be entirely withstood. On 30th July, Gordon sent a message in which he declared his retreat to be impossible.

On 5th August, Mr. Gladstone asked and obtained a vote of credit. Then, and not until then, were the preparations for war begun in England. Having decided, upon the advice of Lord Wolseley, to follow the Nile route instead of the Souakim-Berber route, the Government ordered 800 boats. These were 30 feet long, having six feet six inches beam, two feet six inches draught, fitted with 12 oars, two masts and lug sails; each designed to carry two boatmen and 10 soldiers with provisions, arms and ammunition. Eight steam pinnaces and two stern-wheel paddle-boats were also fitted out; the Nile steamers belonging to the Egyptian Government were taken over; and 380 *voyageurs* from Canada were engaged.

The total force of troops selected numbered 7,000. Messrs. Thomas Cook & Son contracted to transport the whole expedition to above the Second Cataract. Lord Wolseley was appointed commander-in-chief; General Sir Redvers Buller was chief of staff; General Earle was given command of a brigade; special service officers were: Colonels Sir Charles Wilson, Brackenbury, Harrison, Henderson, Maurice, Lord Anson (Royle, *The Egyptian Campaigns*). Lord Charles Beresford was attached to Lord Wolseley's staff.

Even now, the Government failed to recognise the plain facts of the case. Their instructions to Lord Wolseley were that the main object of the expedition was to rescue General Gordon. Her Majesty's Ministers considered that it might be practicable to achieve his release without going to Khartoum, and that in any case it was desirable to avoid any fighting so far as possible.

When Lord Wolseley started from Cairo on 27th September, 1884, the advance was already going rapidly forward. Under the direction of Sir Evelyn Wood and Commander Hammill, a number of the whaler boats had been transported to Wady Haifa, which is nearly 900 miles from Khartoum, the total length of the Nile route being 1,650 miles. Along the river, up to Wady Haifa and a little beyond to Sarras, bases of supply had been established; an advance guard was already at New Dongola, about 100 miles above Wady Haifa, under the command of General Sir Herbert Stewart, he who afterwards led the Desert Column.

Arriving at Wady Haifa on 5th October, Lord Wolseley received news that Colonel J. S. Stewart, Mr Power, British Consul at Khartoum and correspondent of *The Times*, M. Herbin, French Consul, and a party of Greek and Egyptian refugees, who had left Khartoum in the steamer *Abbas*, had all been slain. Stewart had with him Gordon's papers, which, of course, were taken by the *Mahdi's* men.

On the 8th October a letter from M. Herbin was received at Cairo. It was dated from Khartoum, 29th July, 1884, and stated that there were then provisions for two months in the place. The time had thus expired—and M. Herbin had been murdered—ere the letter arrived.

A temporary base was formed at Wady Haifa; and bases of supplies were established along the river up to New Dongola. By means of extraordinary exertions, boats and steamers were hauled up to Dongola through the rapids. Lord Wolseley formed a Camel Corps of 1,500 men, consisting of four regiments, Heavy Cavalry, Light Cavalry, Guards, and Mounted Infantry, with a detachment of Royal Marines.

Early in November, a general advance was made from Wady Haifa. Wolseley arrived at Dongola on 3rd November. Two days previously, on 1st November, Sir Evelyn Baring had received a message from Gordon, dated 13th July, saying that he could hold out for four months. The limit, therefore, had nearly been reached by the time the expedition was leaving Wady Haifa, 900 miles from Khartoum.

Lord Wolseley, early in November, considered that it would take to the end of the year to concentrate his forces at Ambukol, just above Old Dongola. He returned to Wady Haifa to expedite progress; and by the middle of December headquarters were established at Korti, and by Christmas the greater part of the force was concentrated there. During the whole of this period, Wolseley's army must be figured as a river of men flowing along the river Nile, the infantry struggling up in boats, the mounted men toiling along the banks; the stream of men banking up at headquarters, the military front, which is steadily pushed forward from Wady Haifa to New Dongola, from New Dongola to Old Dongola 60 to 70 miles farther up, from Old Dongola to Korti.

On 17th November a letter was received from Gordon saying that he could hold out for forty days from the date of the superscription,

4th November, 1884, thus leaving Wolseley barely four weeks to accomplish a task needing as many months. On 28th November another letter from Gordon, dated 9th September, gave the relief expedition four months, thus leaving Wolseley five weeks from the date upon which the letter was received. It was now clear that the expedition could not reach Khartoum in time. (*Vide The Desert March to Relieve Gordon: the Nile Expedition 1884-5* by Alex Macdonald & Bennet Burleigh; Leonaur 2014.)

When Lord Wolseley, towards the end of December, had his forces concentrated at Korti, he decided to divide them into two columns, the Desert Column and the Nile Column. The reasons for his scheme can only be clearly apprehended by a reference to the map. At Korti, the Nile turns northeast, looping back again, and resuming its southward course at Metemmeh. A straight line drawn across the Bayuda Desert from Korti to Metemmeh is the short cut. This was the route given to the Desert Column. The Nile Column was to proceed up the loop of the river to Hamdab, there to avenge the murder of Colonel Stewart and his party, to proceed higher up to Berti, and thence to secure the bend of the river and to open up the desert route back to Korosko, below Wady Haifa, and from Korosko it was intended to attack Berber, and thence to join forces with the Desert Column at Metemmeh.

The Nile Column, numbering about 3,000 men, under the command of Major-General Earle, Brigadier-General Brackenbury being second in command, left Korti on 28th December, 1884.

The Desert Column was placed under the command of General Sir Herbert Stewart. With him was Colonel Sir Charles Wilson, who was instructed to take a body of troops from Metemmeh to Khartoum. The column consisted of sections of the Camel Corps, a company of the Royal Engineers, a detachment of the 19th Hussars, detachments of the Commissariat and Medical Corps, and the Naval Brigade, which was placed under the command of Lord Charles Beresford. The total force numbered 73 officers, 1,032 non-commissioned officers and men, 2,099 camels, and 40 horses. The Desert Column left Korti on 30th December, 1884. It was, in fact, a forlorn hope.

(The writer desires to acknowledge the use he has made of the excellent narrative of events contained in *The Egyptian Campaigns*, by the Hon. Charles Royle.)

CHAPTER 7

How We Brought the Boats Through the Great Gate

In January, 1884, General Gordon was entrusted by the British and Egyptian Governments with the impossible task of evacuating the Soudan and of organising its future internal administration, in the face of a vast horde of armed fanatics. In April, the investment of Khartoum, in which Gordon was shut up, was complete. In May, preparations for war were begun in England and in Egypt. It was not, however, until 8th August that Lord Hartington informed General Stephenson, commanding the British Army of Occupation in Egypt, that measures would be taken to relieve Gordon. During the same month the whale-boats for the Nile route were ordered. On 26th August General Stephenson was informed that Lord Wolseley would command the expedition.

In August, while I was staying with the Duke of Fife at Mar Lodge, I was appointed to Lord Wolseley's Staff.

I sailed with Lord Wolseley and the rest of his Staff. We arrived at Alexandria on 9th September, 1884, and went on to Cairo, where we lodged in the Palace on the Shoobra Road. Here were Lord Wolseley, General Sir Redvers Buller, Colonel Swaine, Major Wardrop, and Lord Edward Fitzgerald, A.D.C. to Buller. Sir Evelyn Wood and Commander Hammill were already up the Nile organising transport and supply. General Sir Herbert Stewart and General Earle were at Wady Haifa.

It is not my intention to relate the history of the war, which has been admirably recorded in the various works dealing with the subject; but rather to narrate my personal experiences during the campaign. And the reader will also be left to his own consideration of the contemporary affairs of the great world: the marrying and giving in marriage, losses and gains, desires foiled and ambitions achieved,

STEEL STERN-WHEEL STEAMER FOR THE NILE EXPEDITION

NILE BOATS IN SAIL

the shifts and intrigues and gossip of domestic politics, the portentous manoeuvres upon the clouded stage of international drama: all of which, to the sailors and soldiers of the forlorn hope strung along the gigantic reaches of the Nile, toiling and fighting in the desert, went by as though it had never been. It is an old story now; very many of my gallant comrades have passed away; but the record of their courage and endurance remains, and shall remain.

When we arrived in Cairo there were already 29 naval officers and 190 men, divided into several sections, at work along the Nile. These were sent by Admiral Lord John Hay, commander-in-chief in the Mediterranean. In addition, the Admiralty had appointed two or three senior officers, among whom was Captain Boardman (afterwards Admiral F. R. Boardman, C.B.). At Lord Wolseley's request, Boardman was placed in command of the whole naval contingent, which had not hitherto been under either a naval officer in chief command or the military authority. My own position with regard to the naval contingent was simply that of Lord Wolseley's representative.

While we were in Cairo, I purchased for £24 my famous racing camel *Bimbashi*. Buller also bought a camel, and we rode together daily. He used to laugh till he nearly fell out of his saddle, when my camel ran away with me through and over foot-passengers, donkeys, carriages and dogs. I might haul *Bimbashi's* head round till it was under my knee, and he was looking astern, and still he charged onwards.

The whale-boats designed to transport the expedition were then arriving in large numbers. The total number was 800. They were similar to the man-of-war 30-foot whaler, but fuller in the body to enable them to carry more weight. Each boat was 30 feet long, with six feet six inches beam, and two feet six inches draught, fitted for 12 oars, and two masts with lug sails, and capable of carrying 10 soldiers, two boatmen (Canadian *voyageurs*), 1,000 rations and ammunition.

There was a strong current when the boats were struggling up the Nile, that one of them, manned by a sergeant and eight soldiers, but without a *voyageur* on board, having run athwart a rock and upset, a soldier observed to the sergeant that "the cove who sent nine men in a boat with 1,000 rations must have been this here journey before!"

There were also to be provided eight steam pinnaces, two stern-wheel paddle boats, and a number of hired Egyptian Government steamers. The whale-boats as they arrived were sent, first, by rail and river to Assiout. Thence they were towed to Assouan, where is the First Cataract. Here they were either railed on trucks, or hauled through the rapids to Shellal, eight miles up. From Shellal to Wady Haifa, 200 miles farther, was plain sailing. At Wady Haifa is the Second Cataract and the formidable rapid of Bab-el-Kebir, or the "Great Gate."

Early in September I was ordered by Lord Wolseley to go up the Nile, overhauling the arrangements for the water transport, right up to Wady Haifa, which would be the temporary military base. I went by train from Cairo to Assiout, the hottest journey I had ever endured. India was nothing to it. The desert gathered itself up to destroy me. Any little spot upon my person which was not deep in desert was a fly-bazaar. But at Assiout a cold shower-bath paid for all. Here I investigated the transport arrangements made by Captain Boardman, and found them excellent. I may say at once that the whole of Captain Boardman's work was admirable, and that his management throughout the campaign was marked by the greatest good feeling, tact, and patience.

I left Assiout in one of Messrs. Cook's steamers, the *Fersaat*, which had the appearance of a boat and the manners of a kangaroo. She was loosely concocted of iron and leaked at every rivet; she squealed and grunted; her boiler roared like a camel; she bounded as she went. Her *reis* (captain and pilot) was a sorrowful old Mohammedan, whose only method of finding out if the shoals and sands were still in the same place was by running upon them; and his manner of getting off them was to cry "*Allah Kerim!*" ("God is great!") and to beat his poor old forehead on the deck. In the meantime, one of his Arabs, tastefully attired in a long blue night-gown, an enormous pair of drawers, and decorated elastic-sided boots, stripped and jumped overboard and pushed the boat, and while he pushed, he chanted a dirge.

As the boat began to move, he made sounds which suggested that he was about to be violently sick but could not quite manage it satisfactorily, although encouraged thereto by the loud objurgations of the two stokers. When he clambered back on deck, he put on the decorated boots and walked about in them till he was dry enough to dress; while the *reis* gave thanks to his Maker, and the two stokers, men who knew nothing and feared nothing, piled wood on the furnaces and drove the boat along again.

If anyone walked from port to starboard or touched the helm, the boat rolled over, and until the next roll maintained a list of ten degrees, so that I was frequently shot off the locker upon which I was trying to sleep, landing upon the top of José, my Maltese interpreter, and followed by field-glasses, filter, sword and boots. The mosquito-curtains carried away, and the mosquitoes instantly attacked in force, driving me nearly mad with loss of blood, irritation, and rage. My only comfort was a pneumatic life-belt, which had been sent to me by Lady Charles, and which I used as a pillow.

So, we struggled along against the stream for the 330 miles to Assouan; and the weather was not too hot, and the nights were cool, and the banks were fringed with date-palms, and every night the sun sank from the intense blue of the zenith, laced with long-drawn clouds of rose, to the lucent green low in the west, and the sand turned to gold colour and rose, until the sun dropped suddenly out of sight and all turned grey like ashes. Then a cold little wind sprang up out of the desert and the night deepened into the velvet dark flashing with a myriad stars.

On 23rd September I came to Assouan: reorganised the postal service to bring two mails a week by steamlaunch: made arrangements for the rapid working of the water transport generally, ready for the time of pressure, and sent an urgent request for flexible wire hawsers, as I was sure they would be urgently required.

Leaving Assouan on 24th September, I arrived at Wady Haifa on the 27th. Here were Sir Evelyn Wood and his Staff; among whom was my old friend Zohrab Pasha. I was immediately set to work trying camels, as I had become acquainted with these singular animals in India.

Upon the day of my arrival, I went out with a young officer in the Mounted Infantry. His camel blundered over an irrigation ditch, and flung my young friend head over heels into the mud, where he sat looking sadly up into the face of his steed, which was complaining, as camels do, making a peculiar mumbling noise like an old woman kept waiting for her tea. Having been restored to his seat, this unfortunate youth immediately rode too close to the river and incontinently fell into a deep mud hole from which he had to be dug out.

On 5th October Lord Wolseley arrived at Wady Haifa, as cheery as usual, and took up his quarters in a *dahabieh*. Sir Redvers Buller and Zohrab Pasha were also dwelling in *dahabiehs*. I was attached to Sir Evelyn Wood's mess, Sir Evelyn being in charge of communications. I lived in a small bell tent close to the river, chiefly furnished with a penny whistle, a photograph of Lady Charles, my letters from home, and a stag beetle big enough to carry me to hounds, which I generally had to chase from my bed.

Upon Lord Wolseley's arrival we heard the rumour of the murder of Colonel Stewart at El-Kamar, and of the slaying of his companions.

Ultimately, the news was confirmed. Stewart, with three steamers, had left Khartoum on 10th September. After shelling the forts at Berber, two of the steamers returned; while Stewart, in the *Abbas*, which was towing two boats carrying refugees, went on to Abu Hamid, where the natives opened a heavy fire. The boats were cast adrift and their passengers captured. Stewart went on; his steamer was wrecked near the village of Hebbeh, at which, having been induced to land by treachery, Stewart, M. Herbin, French Consul at Khartoum, Mr. Power, *Times* correspondent, and a number of Greeks and Egyptians, were slain. It was a pitiful end to all Colonel Stewart's gallant service with Gordon.

During the first part of my time at Wady Haifa I was engaged under Lord Wolseley's instructions in the inspection of the transport up and down the river, often riding more than forty miles in a day upon a camel. Wady Haifa was then being formed into the base camp preparatory to the general advance: and troops and stores were arriving daily. The railway ran along the east bank of the river to Sarras, 33 miles distant.

One day, when Sir Evelyn Wood and a party of soldiers were going by train to Sarras, and Commander Hammill and I were accompanying them, the engine broke down halfway. The Egyptian engineer and stoker being helpless, Hammill and I examined the locomotive, Hammill taking the top part, while I lay on my back underneath, close to the furnace, where the sensation was like being baked in an oven. The bearings were overheated, a lubricating tube having become unscrewed. After two hours' hard work, we managed to reverse the tube end for end and to refix it.

Sir Evelyn Wood helped to pull me from under the engine, and laughed till he cried. I was covered with black grease from top to toe, and my clothes were scorched to tatters. Hammill was in no better case, his suit being drenched with oil. The spectacle may have been very amusing to the general; but neither Hammill nor I had more than two suits, and here was one of them destroyed entirely.

By the 5th October, when Lord Wolseley arrived at Wady Haifa, Sir Herbert Stewart had been for several days at Dongola with 250 Mounted Infantry, who were transported in *nuggars* (native boats) from Sarras. The whaleboats were arriving daily at Wady Haifa, the first boat having been hauled through the rapids on 25th September, and by the 5th October there were 103 whalers assembled at Wady Haifa. At Wady Haifa is the Second Cataract, at the lower end of which is the gorge of Bab-el-Kebir, the Great Gate. Between Wady Haifa and Dal are the cataracts of Samneh, Attireh, Ambigol, Tangour and Akasha.

At intervals of about 33 miles from Sarras to (New) Dongola, stations were established with commissariat depots. The transport of troops and stores from the base camp at Wady Haifa to Dongola consisted of the steamers, whale-boats, and *nuggars* along the river, the train from Wady Haifa to Sarras, from Sarras to Ambigol by camel, thence by water. The Camel Corps marched along the east bank to Dongola. It was composed of four regiments, Heavy, Light, Guards, and Mounted Infantry, each being composed of detachments from cavalry and infantry regiments, each detachment consisting of two officers, two sergeants, two corporals, one bugler, and 38 men; total, 94 officers, 1,700 N.C.O.'s and men.

Such, in brief, was the condition of affairs early in October (1884), when I was stationed at the Second Cataract at Wady Haifa. Here the Nile divides into two, flowing on either side of a group of rocks and islands for about 20 miles, and at the other (or upper) end of the group of rocks and islands, on the east (or left) bank, is the sickle-shaped gorge of Bab-el-Kebir. At this time, although the river was falling, the roar of the torrent pouring through the Bab was so tremendous, that no voice could be heard, and we communicated with one another by semaphore. When I left the Bab, goats were feeding in the bed of the river.

Lord Wolseley told me that he was informed that it was impossible to haul the steamers up the Second Cataract, and asked me if I could do it.

I replied that nothing was impossible until it was proved to be impossible; and that, in the case under consideration, I would admit the impossibility when I had smashed two steamers in trying to get them through; while if I smashed only one, I might thereby get experience which would enable me to succeed with the other.

The steamers were hauled through successfully while the Bab-el-Kebir was still full and roaring, the current being so powerful that the steamers forging against it trembled like a whip.

Some 4,000 natives were put on the hawser of the first steamer; and as they hauled her up, she had but a foot's clearance between her sides and the rocks. The torrent flung her against them, and if she had not been defended by timber and mats, she would have been smashed to pieces. About the middle of the gorge the natives could move her no farther. Whereupon they cried to *Allah* to strengthen them, and to order the rope to pull harder and to slacken the water. But as their prayers availed not, I eased the steamer back again, and put

The Camel Corps of the Desert Column

about 1,500 British soldiers on the hawser. They did not pray; indeed, their language was as it were the reverse of prayer; but they dragged the steamer right through. Theologically speaking, the victory should have gone to the natives. I put the problem to a bishop, but he was unable to solve it.

The task of hauling the whalers through the Second Cataract was at first entrusted to Koko, the native pilot of Bab-el-Kebir. His method was to take a line, dive with it into the rapids, and carry it across the river. The line was frequently torn from him by the current, and many of the boats were stove in against the rocks.

I designed a scheme of haulage, and was eventually placed by Lord Wolseley in charge of the whole of the water transport from Wady Haifa to Gemai, a stretch of about 17 miles. At Gemai was established a dockyard, where damaged boats were repaired and equipped for the rest of the voyage.

My scheme for hauling the boats consisted of a stout standing guess-warp rigged as nearly as possible at right angles to the course of the boat to be hauled, and secured at either end to rock or tree; one end of a short hawser was hooked to the guess-warp, so that it could move freely up and down it, and a block was secured to the other end. Through the block was rove a towing rope proper, one end secured to the boat, and the working party on land tailing on to the other. As the course of the river shifted, the guess warp was moved; the whole passage being accomplished by a series of these operations.

In certain places two blocks were used, a standing block and a pendant block, a pendant being rove through the standing block, one end secured to the pendant block, men hauling on the other end; and through the pendant block was rove the hauling line, one end secured to the boat, men hauling on the other upon the bank opposite to that on which were the pendant crew. By hauling on the hauling line, then easing the pendant, and then hauling again on the hauling line, the boat was brought clear of the Cataract and hauled round the corner into smooth water.

Each boat was supplied with two poles for punting and a long line for tracking, besides oars and sails.

The whole equipment of the boats was organised by Sir Redvers Buller, who utilised his experience of the Red River expedition, and nothing could have better served its purpose.

The *nuggars*, or native boats, were bought near Assouan, and were then brought up to Wady Haifa, whence they were hauled through the Cataract, then loaded with stores and sent on up river. It was of the utmost importance that they should be dispatched as quickly as possible; for an army moves on its stomach, and the *nuggars* carried the wherewithal. Their sails, being invariably rotten, were blown to pieces in the Cataracts. They were constantly crashing into the rocks, which made holes in them, when they were hauled by main force to the shore, where a dock was excavated in the sand to receive them. Here they were repaired and thence dispatched up river.

A *nuggar* would come sailing along, when there was a sudden crash, the bluejacket at the helm was pitched headlong into the bottom of the boat, while the sail split into ribbons, and the native crew embraced the mast crying that *Allah* was great!

When the whale-boats came along, their passage was so arranged that a regiment, or part of a regiment, was kept together; the distribution being maintained all up the river, so that a homogeneous body could be landed at any moment for attack or defence if necessary.

So furious was the torrent, that whoso fell into it seldom rose again, unless he were one of the expert Dongola divers.

The men coming up in the boats, who had done and suffered much before reaching Wady Haifa, had repaired their trousers with biscuit tins. I overheard the following dialogue between one of these tin-bottomed weary heroes and a comrade on the bank:

"Hullo, Bill, 'ow are you getting on?"

"Me? I've been pulling on this here ruddy river for about two years. 'Ow far is it to Gemai?"

"About fifteen miles, mate."

"O my Gawd! Is there an 'orspital there?"

Late in October, the *voyageurs* arrived, a fine body of men, 380 strong.

Being acquainted with rapids and understanding their navigation, the *voyageurs* were invaluable in bringing the boats through the long and difficult reaches of the Nile up to Wady Haifa, and from Wady Haifa up to Korti. The task could never have been accomplished in the time, and the losses of boats would have been heavier, had it not been for the *voyageurs*.

As the boats came through the Bab or across the portage, the *voyageurs* took charge of them and sailed them up to Gemai. Here they were overhauled and fully equipped, the soldiers were embarked, and away they went up river.

By the 6th November, 60 boats had left Gemai with the Sussex

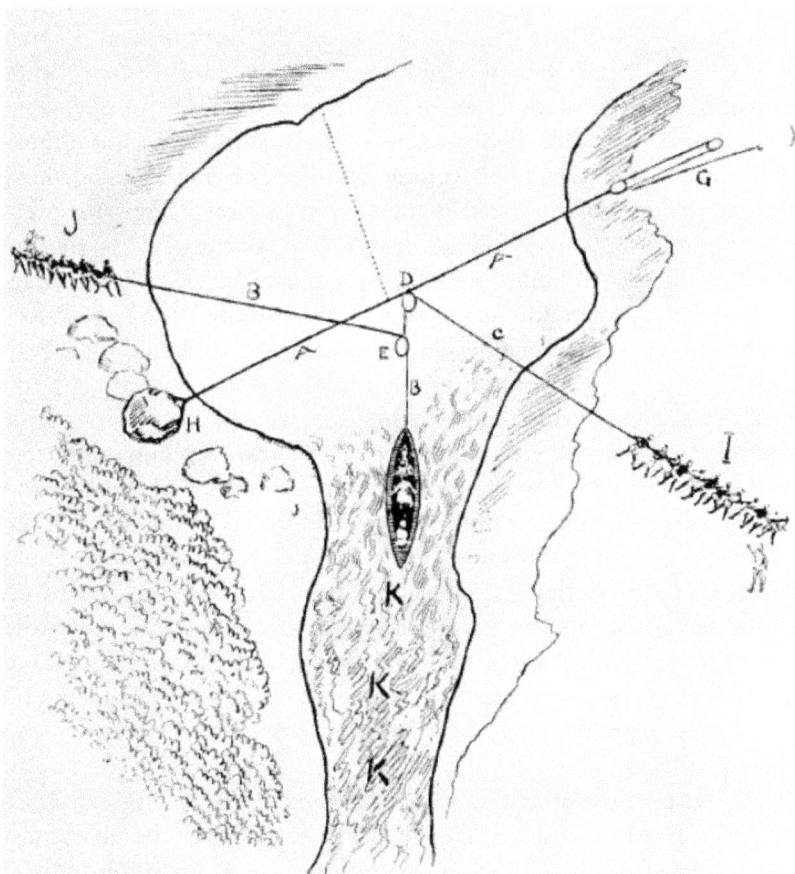

THE AUTHOR'S METHOD OF HAULING BOATS THROUGH THE BAB-EL-KEBIR

AA, HAWSER; BB, HAULING LINE; C, GILGUY; J AND I, MEN HAULING; H, FIXED POINT; G, PURCHASE FOR SETTING TAUT

AFTER A DRAWING MADE ON THE SPOT BY THE AUTHOR

regiment on board. The river was then falling so swiftly that a new course for the boats must be found almost every day. Hitherto the boats had been passed through the Cataract almost without a scratch or the loss of a single article of gear. Now the rocks began to show through the surf in the Bab.

A boat was smashed. We caught her lower down; and with 200 men portaged her over a rocky hill, across the neck of land formed by the curve of the Bab, then laid her keel upwards across two other boats, and so floated, took her up to Gemai dockyard. I was the more pleased with this piece of salvage, because everyone said it was impossible to save the boat. The last nine boats, after being emptied of all gear, were hauled clean over the rocks by main force. They came prettily lipping through the boiling torrent from rock to rock, taking the blows upon keel and bilge pieces, so that they were scarcely damaged.

Early in October, foreseeing that, as the water fell, the Bab-el-Kebir would become impracticable, I had designed a scheme for a portage. The alternative would have been to entrain the boats from Wady Haifa to Sarras, an expedient which, as the whole of the train service was required to carry provisions, would have involved immense delay.

My plan was to haul the boats up to the entrance of the Bab and then to carry them across the neck of land formed by the curve of the Bab, a distance of 2,488 yards, which required 400 men, who should be divided into sections of 40 to each boat. The boat was hauled on shore, her masts, oars, and poles laid on the ground to serve as bearers; the boat was laid on these keel uppermost, and was then lifted and carried, the masts, oars, and poles resting on the men's shoulders, and other men supporting the boat by resting thwarts and gunwale on their shoulders.

My scheme was at first received with incredulity by all except Lord Wolseley. But I made a trial trip with 30 men, and had the boat across the portage, including six stoppages for rest, and in the water with all her gear without a scratch, in an hour and twenty minutes. The passage of Bab-el-Kebir, low as the water had become, would have taken at least six hours, with great risk of disaster.

Now, having hauled the last nine boats through, over the rocks, the portage scheme came into operation; and on the 6th November I closed the Bab, and used the portage, by means of which alone it was made possible to continue the supply of boats at the same rate. Thenceforward we were able to put the boats through quicker than they were supplied.

Many of the boats were poisonous to handle, as their matting was infested with scorpions.

My dwelling was at first a tent at Wady Haifa, and afterwards a hut on the bank beside the Bab-el-Kebir. It stood within six feet of the roaring river, in a grove of mimosa. The camels lunched daily upon the long sharp thorns of the mimosa, apparently relishing these spines as a form of Worcester sauce.

Rising at daylight, every day I covered some thirty miles up and down the shore of the Cataract, superintending operations from dawn till dark. I rode one of my camels, *Bimbashi* or *Ballyhooly* or *Beelzebub*, or my donkey, *County Waterford*, so named because the second time I contested him I lost my seat: a political allegory. Being short of both officers and men, my presence was required everywhere at once. By haulage and portage a perpetual procession of whaleboats and *nuggars* was kept moving up to the dockyard at Gemai.

From Wady Haifa to the Bab the Cataract was divided into reaches, a post being stationed at each. At the first reach were Peel of the 2nd Life Guards and 200 Dongola men; at the Naval Camp, on the second reach, were Lieutenant Colbourne and 350 Dongola men; at Palm Tree Camp, in the third reach, were an Egyptian officer and 100 Dongola men; for the portage at Bab-el-Kebir I had 500 men of the 2nd Egyptian battalion under their colonel, and another of their officers, Shakespeare of the marines, who had been with me in the *Thunderer*. All along the Cataract were stationed small parties of carpenters and sailmakers in order that damages should be repaired on the spot. Living with me was Colonel Grant, who was in command of all the Dongola men. Later, the Canadian *voyageurs* camped beside my hut.

By means of the distribution of work, each section being placed under a responsible officer, progress speedily became three times as fast. Officers and men worked magnificently. I was proud of the old navy.

The routine for the bluejackets was: Turn out 4.30 a.m., breakfast; walk seven to ten miles through the desert along the river, often having to retrace their steps to help a boat in distress; work all day till sunset, no spell for dinner, which consisted of biscuit; at sunset, walk seven miles back to camp, supper and turn in. The officers walked with the men, giving their camels to the men who suffered from sore feet. Officers and men were burned as black as the natives.

Until my arrival, the nine naval officers and the doctor had been living at the naval camp nine miles from Wady Haifa, without a single servant or a cook. They were allowed neither servants nor the money with which to hire natives. But nothing could exceed the kindness and goodwill of General Buller, who at once granted all my requests, and if I found it necessary to order first and report afterwards, sanctioned my requisitions.

I had with me in my hut for a time F. H. Pollen, who could dive and swim better than the Dongola men, using like them a blown-up goatskin. The constant immersion brought on an attack of dysentery. I kept him in bed, taking away his clothes so that he could not get up, and doctored him till he recovered.

At this time, I acted as doctor to the men under me. Every case of sickness was reported to me at once. If the patient suffered from diarrhoea, I exhibited castor oil. A petty officer having been thus treated, said he felt easier. I asked him if he would like another dose, and he said he would like it. The same night he died. I sent his body on a camel to the nearest medical officer, who found seventeen date-stones in his stomach. I had the sorry consolation of knowing that the poor fellow must have died in any event.

On the 17th November, Lord Wolseley, returning from Dongola, arrived suddenly at Wady Haifa, where he remained for twenty-four hours, afterwards returning to Dongola. All we knew was that he had come to press matters forward. History relates how that on the 17th November, Wolseley received a letter from Gordon dated 4th November, in which Gordon wrote:

We can hold out forty days with ease; after that it will be difficult.

In reply Wolseley telegraphed from Wady Haifa:

Yours of 4th just received 17th; the first I have had from you. I shall be at Kasr Dongola in four days.

Wolseley at the same time informed Lord Hartington that while the news would not affect his plans, it seemed to show that Gordon's relief could not be accomplished without fighting.

Lord Wolseley made no announcement on the subject at the time, merely telling General Buller and myself that we were to stay where we were for the present. Our impression was that Wolseley had abandoned the idea of making a dash across the desert from Korti to Metemmeh.

At that date, 17th November, we had more than 200 boats ready to embark troops at Gemai, from which twenty to thirty boats were being dispatched daily. Nearly 200 boats had already gone, carrying detachments of the Essex, Stafford, and Cornwall Regiments, the Engineers, and Commissariat. About 200 more boats had still to pass the Cataract. I was very pleased with the work and behaviour of the 2nd battalion of the Egyptian Army, which was working the portage. I expressed my satisfaction to them, and gave every man a quarter of a pound of native tobacco, whereupon they declared with one voice that, "if God was willing, they would go to hell with my Excellency."

At about this time I received a private intimation from Lord Wolseley that, when the general advance began, he intended to place me in command of a naval brigade.

By 22nd November, 549 boats had been passed through the Second Cataract, 166 of which had been hauled through the Bab-el-Kebir, the rest portaged. Of the whole number of boats, only three were smashed; and very few received any damage. Accidents were few, although the work was dangerous. On 21st November a *voyageur* was drowned. Three *voyageurs* went overboard, and two were saved by catching hold of a rope. The third scorned the rope, relying upon his ability to swim, and was never seen again. Up to that date five men altogether had been drowned, two soldiers, two Canadians, and one native. Later, another native, and he an Esneh swimmer, was drowned. The river was extraordinarily fatal. Not one man who went under upon falling overboard was saved. The natives always used to do their best to keep on the surface.

Lord Wolseley was so good as warmly to commend the work done on the Second Cataract; and Sir Redvers Buller, who at first declared the portage scheme to be impossible of execution, generously expressed his appreciation of its success.

Having shot a little alligator, I skinned it myself. The Arab camel-man in my service, who spoke French, argued with me in that language for a long time that an alligator had no tongue, but fed by suction, like a snipe. As I had cut out the tongue of my little alligator, I knew it had one; but my Arabian naturalist refused to be persuaded.

At this time and afterwards while I was in Egypt, my servant, interpreter and cook was the excellent José Salvatro, a Maltese. If he happened to be absent, I conveyed my instructions to the natives through my French-speaking camel-man, in French. Between my French and his French and his Arabic, I used to wonder how the meaning filtered through; but I have a note in my diary that "it comes all right, the natives are cheery fellows and work capitally with me, and a good smack upon the 'sit-upon' of a lazy one keeps the whole lot going."

Towards the end of November, I was living alone in my hut on the Bab-el-Kebir, attended only by a bluejacket and the faithful José, who ceased not from scrubbing and washing, so that I was never a day without clean things, an inestimable comfort in that climate. Here I was haunted by an Arab maniac who dwelt in some indiscoverable antre of the rocks. At night I heard him howling to himself.

In the daytime, he ran here and there, his only garment being the dust he cast upon his shaven head, crying upon *Allah*. He ate sand and offal, a diet which left him hungry, for he would come to my tent for food, which I gave him. He seemed to know me in a vague way. I gave him some calico to cover his nakedness withal, but he tore the stuff into fragments and ate them. One day he rushed into my tent, clawed some mutton-broth out of the cooking-pot with his horrible hands and crammed it boiling hot into his mouth. I was obliged forcibly to eject him lest he should take the whole; but I had no stomach for the rest. My fear was lest he should burst in at night and I should be obliged in self-defence to shoot him. Eventually, José lost patience, seized a huge wood-axe, and chased the maniac for a mile. The poor wretch ran like a hare and vanished into his hole in the rocks.

I made a match with Colonel Brocklehurst, head of the Remount Department, to ride my camel, the bold *Bimbashi*, against any one of Brocklehurst's camels, for £25. The course was six miles long across the desert, from Peel's Camp at the beginning of the Cataract to Sir Evelyn Wood's flagstaff at Wady Haifa. Brocklehurst's rider was his interpreter, a lean rat of an Arab *sheikh*, who was absolutely certain he would win. His camel was the favourite of Wood's mess and was reputed to be the best in Egypt. The betting was fifty to one against me. But I had been riding *Bimbashi* 30 miles or so a day, and we were both in fine hard condition.

The *sheikh* started at a gallop. First his turban, then his goatskin saddle-rug, carried away. Both rider and camel were blowing and perspiring ere they had run three miles. For the first two and a half miles I waited on the *sheikh*, then came away and won in a canter half a mile ahead. At the finish the troops lined up and made a course for us. Thus, I won my first camel race, owner up. No one was better pleased than my old friend Colonel Brocklehurst.

Bimbashi (according to my *journal*) covered the six miles in a little over eighteen minutes. That gallant steed had already been ridden the nine miles from my camp to the starting-point; and when I rode him back in the evening, he was so fresh that he ran away with me, grumbling loudly, because he was offended at the sight of a dead donkey lying wrong side up beside the railway.

I invented a saddle for camels, and I believe the pattern is still in use. The saddle-tree is a triangular wooden framework, like the gable of a roof. I covered the wood with oakum and canvas; abolished all buckles, made the girths and stirrups of raw hide thongs, and put the stirrups forward, instead of behind. Count Gleichen, in his interesting book, *With the Camel Corps up the Nile,* (republished Leonaur 2010), relates how the saddles and equipment served out to the Camel Corps gave the men infinite trouble and discomfort. The unseasoned wood came to pieces, the straps broke, the water-skins and water-bottles leaked; but one instance of the departmental mismanagement which caused our men so much unnecessary suffering.

By the end of November, the river was falling so swiftly that what was smooth water yesterday was today a frivolous series of waterfalls with a twist in them. Every alteration in the river involved a new device for haulage, and it would alter at three or four places in a mile, and there were 11 miles of rapids. I was generally able to judge by the look of the water when and where it would change its course during the next few hours. In order to avoid the least delay, new arrangements must be devised beforehand; and my mind was so absorbed in these schemes, that I dreamed of them nightly. By that time, I had 1,400 men working under me, whose work must be organised, and stations allocated. The Bab-el-Kebir, that formidable rapid, was now a grazing ground for goats.

I shifted my quarters from the Bab to Wady Haifa, as the difficulties were now all at that end of the Cataract. Peel and Colbourne, in command respectively of the next two reaches, found no day too long and no work too hard.

In order to supervise the whole length of the operations as quickly as possible, I kept one camel, *Ballyhooly,* at the Bab; the big white donkey *County Waterford* half-way there; and *Bimbashi* the bold and *Beelzebub* at Wady Haifa. *Bimbashi* could trot 16 miles in the hour. A Bedouin *sheikh* offered me £35 for him. As I had bought him for £24, I concluded that his vender had stolen him. I won more than his price in the race with Colonel Brocklehurst's Sheikh. While at Wady Haifa, I rode him six miles out in the heavy sand against Sir Evelyn Wood and his A.D.C., who rode horses, and *Bimbashi* beat the horses fair and square.

Lord Wolseley sent me a telegram ordering me to form a naval brigade of 100 men and 10 officers. But as the bluejackets were of inestimable service in getting the remainder of the boats through the Cataract, and fitting them out at Gemai, where the soldiers embarked, he desired to keep them where they were as long as possible. On 27th November, we hoped to get all the boats through during the next five days. Up to that date—the last for which I have a note—687 boats had been passed through the Cataract, with a loss of 4 only; about 27 men of all sorts had been drowned; and 337 boats had left Gemai with troops and stores.

On 6th December the last boat was passed through. On the same day, Sir Evelyn Wood and Sir Redvers Buller received a telegram reporting a block of boats at Ambigol and Dal Cataract; and I was ordered there at a moment's notice.

On 27th September I had arrived at Wady Haifa; on 10th October I schemed the portage; and for eight weeks since that date I had been continuously hard at work passing the boats through the Second Cataract; which the Arabs call "the belly of stone."

CHAPTER 8

Up the Cataracts and across the Desert

To Assiout, in a cloud of dust
We came, and it made us smile,
To see each other's features, till
We washed them in the Nile.
From there, by boat, to Assouan
We came, and every night
Made fast, for the boatmen wouldn't steam
Excepting in daylight.

Songs of the Camel Corps (Sergt. H. Eagle, R.M.C.C.)

On the 6th December, 1884, Peel and Colbourne, my two gallant comrades who had done so splendid a work upon the Second Cataract, quitted the Belly of Stone, embarking in two boats manned by Kroomen. The names of these big black men were Africa, Ginger Red, Bottled Beer, Sampson, Two Glasses and Been-Very-Ill-Twice; and when they were excited, as they nearly always were, they took to the English tongue, and kept us laughing for a week. When the wind was fair and we sailed up against the rapids, the *Kroo* boys were terribly anxious, knowing that if the wind failed we should slide all the way back again.

By this time the whole expedition was moving up river. The conduct of the soldiers was magnificent, achieving wonderful results. Of the sailors, accustomed to the work, and knowing the shortest way of doing things, one expected much—and got even more. It was hard enough for the seamen. Although they, the soldiers, knew nothing of boats, they worked like heroes. And the navigation of the Nile from Gemai to Dal enforced hard continuous toil from dawn to dark day after day. The *voyageurs* did splendid service; the expedition could not have advanced so rapidly without them; and although they knew nothing of sails, being acute adventurous fellows they soon picked up enough knowledge to carry them through.

An officer of cavalry in charge of a convoy of stores on the river worked by Dongola men, describing his adventures with what he called his "peasant crews," pathetically observed: "You know, I know nothing whatever about a boat, or what it ought to do, and I am not ashamed to tell you that the whole time I am sweating with terror. And every night when I go to bed I dream of whirlpools and boiling rapids and then I dream that I am drowned."

But his visions of the night affected neither his nerve nor his indomitable energy.

Our daily routine along the river began at 4.30: all hands turn out, make up tent (if there were one), breakfast, and start, sailing or tracking or rowing according to the state of the river. But whether you sailed or tracked or rowed, before long the river changed and you must row instead of track, or sail instead of row. Then you would come to a difficult place, and you would heave the cargo on shore, and get the empty boat up a fall or a heavy rush of water, and portage the cargo on to the boat. So on to midday, when an hour was allowed for dinner; then at it again, sailing, tracking, rowing, in and out cargo, till sundown. Then haul into the bank and eat bully beef without vegetables. After supper, roll in a blanket and sleep on the soft sand the profound and delicious slumber of weary men.

Occasionally a boat would strike a rock; or at rare intervals an accident would happen, and part of a crew would be lost, and the boat's gear swept away; or a hole would be knocked in the boat, when she would be emptied of gear and cargo, hauled up, and patched. Under these circumstances, the boats often made no more than three or four miles' advance in a day. Overloaded as were many of the boats, they served their purpose admirably well.

At the big Cataracts were stationed working parties, which emptied the boats of gear and cargo, portaged them overland, and hauled the boats through the rapids.

So, we struggled up the broad and rushing river from Gemai to Dal, sailing and towing and rowing, capsized and righting again. And one night a sandstorm waltzed out of the desert and blew away our tent and, with it, knives, forks, slippers, lamp, candles, matches and everything. And the next morning Peel dropped his knife, and in trying to save it he upset our whole breakfast of sardines and coffee into Colbourne's boots. And half my kit was stolen, and I was reduced to one broken pair of boots, and the natives stole my tooth powder and baked bread with it. And we had boils all over us like the man in the Bible, because every little scratch was poisoned by the innumerable flies of Egypt. But we were so busy that nothing mattered.

Fighting every mile of the great river pouring down from Khartoum, we on the Cataracts had no news of Gordon. All we knew was that there was need to hurry, hurry all the way. At such times as the mail from home arrived upon a dyspeptic camel, we got scraps of news of home affairs. People who knew much more than Lord Wolseley, were saying he ought to have taken the Souakim-Berber route instead of the Nile route. I said then, as I say now, he had no choice.

At this time of crisis, when the navy was dangerously inadequate, one political party was screaming denunciations against "legislation by panic." Encouraging to sailors and soldiers sweating on service! But we knew what to expect. I observe that in a private letter written in December, 1884, from the banks of the Nile, at the end of a long day's work with the boats, I said, "Both sides are equally to blame for the defective state of the Navy. Tell —— and —— not to be unpatriotic and make the navy a party question, or they will not do half the good they might."

We came to Ambigol to find the boats had been cleared by Alleyne of the Artillery. I was able to improve the organisation there, and to give help along the river. I was in time to save three boats. At Dal, I laid lines along the centre of the two and a half miles rapid, so that in calm weather the boats could haul themselves through.

In the meantime, the Naval Brigade of which Lord Wolseley had ordered me to take command, had been selected, at my request, by Captain Boardman.

On 19th December, my first division came to Dal. Up they came, all together in line ahead, under all possible sail, using the boat awnings as spinnakers. They had sailed up the rapids where the other boats were tracking; and the soldiers cheered them as they went by. There was not a scratch on any boat, nor a drop of water in any of them. Every cargo was complete in detail, including machine guns, ammunition, oil and stores. Had I not a right to be proud of the seamen? I put an officer at the helm of each boat, and told them to follow me through Dal Cataract; and led them through, so that the same night the boats were reloaded with the gear and cargo which had been portaged, and were going on. The passage of Dal Cataract usually occupied three days.

I sent on the first division, and stayed at Dal to await the arrival of the second, in order to get all my men together. As it happened, I did not see it until it reached Korti. On 21st December it had left Sarras, bringing oil and stores to be used in the Nile steamers of which I was to take charge. For by this time, I had been informed of Lord Wolseley's intention to send the Naval Brigade with the Camel Corps to make a dash across the Bayuda Desert to Metemmeh. The Naval Brigade was then to attack Khartoum in Gordon's steamers, while the Camel Corps attacked it by land.

So, I remained yet a little while at Dal, helping the boats through the Cataract, and camping in the sand. I found a baby scorpion two and a half inches long in my handkerchief. The officer whose tent was next to mine, shared it with a sand-rat, which used to fill his slippers with *dhura* grains every night, and which jumped on and off my knee when I breakfasted with my friend. Actually, there came two or three days when I had nothing to do; and when I could take a hot bath in peace, with the luxury of a cake of carbolic soap, and sit in my little canvas chair, which was, however, speedily stolen.

My poor servant José was suddenly taken with so sharp an attack of fever that he was stricken helpless and could hardly lift a cup to his lips. His pulse was going like a machine gun. He was too ill to be moved on mule-back to the hospital, which was eight miles distant; and I had to doctor him myself I gave him castor-oil, deprived him of all food for twenty-four hours, gave him five grains of quinine every two hours, and plenty of lime-juice to drink; and he was soon well again.

Lord Avonmore, Lieutenant-Colonel J. Alleyne, Captain Burnaby and myself subscribed to a Christmas dinner of extraordinary charm, eaten with the Guards. The menu was:—soup made of bully beef, onions, rice and boiled biscuit, fish from the Nile, stewed bully beef and chicken *à la* as-if-they-had-been-trained-for-long-distance-races-for-a-year, *entremet* of biscuit and jam. Rum to drink.

I should have missed that feast, and should have been on the way to Korti post-haste several days before Christmas, had it not been that a telegram sent by Lord Wolseley to me had been delayed in transmission. On 27th December I received an urgent telegram from General Buller, asking where I was and what I was doing. A week previously Lord Wolseley had telegraphed instructions that I was to proceed to Korti with all speed to arrive with the first division of the Naval Brigade. Having received no orders, I was waiting for the second division so that I might see that it was complete and satisfactory. (It arrived at Dal the day after I left that place in obedience to General Buller's orders.)

From Dal to Korti, as the crow flies, is some 200 miles to the southward; following up the river, which, with many windings, flows north from Korti, the distance is more than half as much again. I was already (by no fault of mine) a week behind; my instructions were to proceed by the shortest possible route by the quickest possible means, camels or steam pinnace; and immediately I received General Buller's telegram I dashed off to the Commissariat. Here I obtained four camels to carry José, myself and my kit to the nearest point at which I could catch a steam pinnace on the river. Also, by riding the first stage of the journey, I could avoid two wide bends of the Nile. The camels were but baggage animals; they all had sore backs; and I could get no proper saddle. I strapped my rug on the wooden framework. We started the same evening at seven o'clock.

The night had fallen when we left behind us the stir of the armed camp and plunged into the deep stillness of the desert. The brilliant moonlight sharply illumined the low rocky hills, and the withered scrub, near and far; the hard gravelly track stretched plainly before us; and the camels went noiselessly forward on their great padded feet. So, hour after hour. It was one o'clock upon the following morning (21st December) when we rode into a dark and silent village. Lighting upon an empty hut, we crawled into it, cooked a little supper, and went to sleep.

Before daylight we were awakened by the noise of voices crying and quarrelling; and there were two black negresses upbraiding us, and beyond them was a group of agitated natives. It appeared that we were desecrating the village mosque. Having soothed the inhabitants, we started. That day we rode from 6 a.m. to 7.30 p.m. with a halt of an hour and a half at midday, travelling 40 miles in twelve hours, good going for baggage camels with sore backs. By that time, I was getting sore, too. We slept that night at Absarat, started the next morning (29th December) at 8.30, and rode to Abu Fatmeh, arriving at 4 p.m. Starting next morning at nine o'clock, we arrived at Kaibur at 5 p.m. Here, to my intense relief, we picked up Colville and his steam pinnace, in which we instantly embarked for Korti,

During the last three days and a half we had been thirty-two hours in the saddle (which, strictly speaking, my camel had not) and a part of my anatomy was quite worn away. I lay down in the pinnace and hoped to become healed.

We did not know it; but the same evening, General Sir Herbert Stewart's Desert Column left Korti upon the great forced march of the forlorn hope.

The pinnace, whose furnaces were burning wood, most of which was wet and green, pounded slowly up river until we met the steamer *Nassifara*, into which I transferred myself. Blissful was the rest in that steamer after my two months' tremendous toil getting the boats through the Bab-el-Kebir and the long ride across the desert. So, I lay in the steamer and lived on the height of diet, fresh meat, milk, butter and eggs, till my tunic hardly held me. I did not then know why Lord Wolseley had sent for me in so great a hurry.

CHAPTER 9

The First March of the Desert Column

NOTE

By the end of December, 1884, the whole of the expedition was in process of concentrating at Korti. At Korti the Nile fetches a wide arc north-eastward. The chord of the arc, running south-eastward, runs from Korti to Metemmeh, and Shendi, which stands on the farther, or east, bank. From Korti to Metemmeh is 176 miles across the desert. Shendi was the rendezvous at which the troops were to meet Gordon's steamers sent down by him from Khartoum. Wolseley's object in sending Lord Charles Beresford with the Naval Brigade was that he should take command of the steamers, which, filled with troops, were to proceed up to Khartoum. The first business of the Desert Column under General Sir Herbert Stewart, was to seize the wells of Jakdul, which lay 100 miles distant from Korti, and to hold them, thus securing the main water supply on the desert route and an intermediate station between Metemmeh and the base at Korti.

Having obtained possession of the wells, the Guards' Battalion was to be left there, while the remainder of the Column returned to Korti, there to be sufficiently reinforced to return to Jakdul, and to complete the march to Metemmeh. Such was the original idea. The reason why sufficient troops and transport were not sent in the first instance, thereby avoiding the necessity of the return of the greater part of the Column to Korti, and its second march with the reinforcements, seems to have been the scarcity of camels.

When the Desert Column made its first march, Lord Charles Beresford and the Naval Brigade were still on their way to Korti. The first division under the command of Lord Charles marched with the Desert Column on its return.

The first Desert Column numbered 73 officers, 1,212 men and natives, and 2091 camels. It consisted of one squadron of the 19th Hussars, Guards' Camel Regiment, Mounted Infantry, Engineers, 1357 camels carrying stores and driven by natives, Medical Staff Corps, and Bearer Company. Personal luggage was limited to 40 lb. a man. An account of the march is given by Count Gleichen, in his pleasant and interesting book (to which the present writer is much indebted) *With the Camel Corps up the Nile.*

Some years previously the route from Korti to Metemmeh had been surveyed by Ismail Pasha, who had intended to run a railway along it from Wady Haifa to Khartoum; and the map then made of the district was in possession of the Column. The enemy were reported to be about; but it was expected that they would be found beyond the Jakdul Wells; as indeed they were.

The Desert Column started from Korti on the afternoon of Tuesday, 30th December, 1884. The hussars escorted a party of native guides and scouted ahead. The column marched the whole of that night, in the light of a brilliant moon, across hard sand or gravel, amid low hills of black rock, at whose bases grew long yellow *savas* grass and mimosa bushes, and in places mimosa trees.

At 8.30 on the morning of the 31st December they halted until 3 p.m., marched till 8.30 p.m., found the wells of Abu Hashim nearly dry, marched on, ascending a stony tableland, and still marching, sang the New Year in at midnight; came to the wells of El Howeiyat, drank them dry and bivouacked until 6 a.m. on the morning of the 1st January, 1885.

All that morning they marched, coming at midday to a plain covered with scrub and intersected with dry watercourses; rested for three hours; marched all that night, and about 7 a.m. on the morning of 2nd January, entered the defile, floored with large loose stones and closed in with steep black hills, leading to the wells of Jakdul. These are deep pools filling clefts in the rock of the hills encompassing the little valley, three reservoirs rising one above the other. Count Gleichen, who was the first man to climb to the upper pools, thus describes the middle pool.

Eighty feet above my head towered an overhanging precipice of black rock; behind me rose another of the same height; at the foot of the one in front lay a beautiful, large ice-green pool, deepening into black as I looked into its transparent depths. Scarlet dragon-flies flitted about in the shade; rocks covered

19TH HUSSARS CROSSING THE DESERT

19TH HUSSARS TAKING ABU-KLEA WELLS

with dark-green weed looked out of the water; the air was cool almost to coldness. It was like being dropped into a fairy grotto, at least so it seemed to me after grilling for days in the sun.

When the Desert Column reached that oasis, they had been on the march for sixty-four hours, with no more than four hours' consecutive sleep. The time as recorded by Count Gleichen was "sixty-four hours, thirty-four hours on the move and thirty broken up into short halts." The distance covered was a little under 100 miles; therefore, the camels' rate of marching averaged as nearly as may be two and three-quarter miles an hour throughout. A camel walks like clock-work, and if he quickens his speed he keeps the same length of pace, almost exactly one yard.

The Guards' Battalion, to which were attached the Royal Marines, with six hussars and 15 engineers remained at the Wells. The rest of the column left Jakdul at dusk of the day upon which they had arrived, to return to Korti, bivouacking that night in the desert.

The detachment at Jakdul made roads, built forts, and laid out the camp for the returning column. On 11th January, a convoy of 1,000 camels carrying stores and ammunition, under the command of Colonel Stanley Clarke, arrived at Jakdul.

In the meantime, on 31st December, the day after which the Desert Column had started for the first time, Lord Wolseley had received a written message from Gordon, "Khartoum all right," dated 14th December. Should it be captured, the message was intended to deceive the captor. The messenger delivered verbal information of a different tenure, to the effect that Gordon was hard pressed and that provisions were becoming very scarce.

At the time of the starting of the Desert Column upon its second march, when it was accompanied by the first division of the Naval Brigade under the command of Lord Charles Beresford, and by other reinforcements, the general situation was briefly as follows.

The River Column, which was intended to clear the country along the Nile, to occupy Berber, and thence to join the Desert Column at Metemmeh, was assembling at Hamdab, 52 miles above Korti. It was commanded by General Earle. The four steamers sent down the river from Khartoum by General Gordon in October, were at Nasri Island, below the Shabloka Cataract, half-way between Khartoum and Metemmeh, which are 98 miles apart. Korti and Berber, as a glance at the map will show, occupy respectively the left and right corners of the base of an inverted pyramid, of which Metemmeh is the apex, while Khartoum may be figured as at the end of a line 98 miles long depending from the apex. The Desert Column traversed one side of the triangle, from Korti to Metemmeh; the River Column was intended to traverse the other two sides.

THE NILE
from Wady Halfa to Khartoum

2nd Cataract · Wady Halfa
Gemai
Sarras
Semneh
Ambigol
Tangour
Dal · Akasha

Oxford
Thames
Reading · Windsor
Salisbury
Southampton
Portsmouth

Kaïbur

Part of England on same scale
for comparison

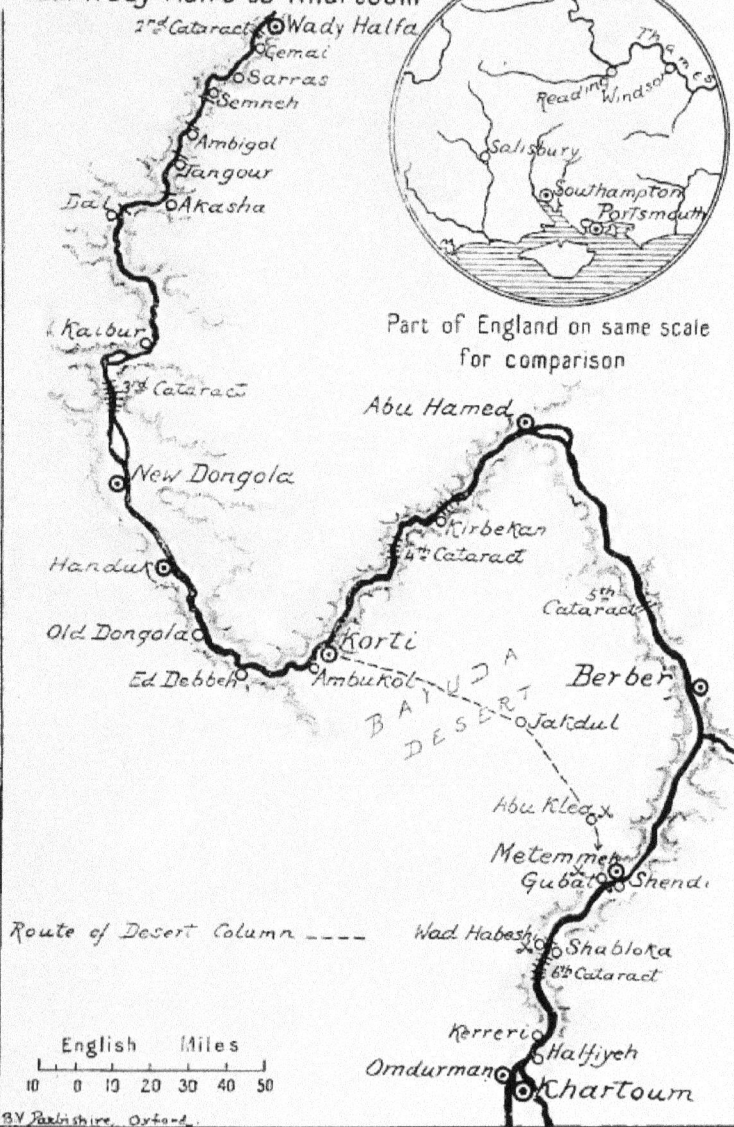

3rd Cataract

Abu Hamed

New Dongola

Kirbekan
4th Cataract

5th Cataract

Handuk

Old Dongola

Korti

Berber

Ed Debbeh · Ambukol

BAYUDA
DESERT

Jakdul

Abu Klea ×

Metemmeh
Gubat · Shendi

Route of Desert Column ____

Wad Habesh · Shabloka
6th Cataract

English   Miles

10 0 10 20 30 40 50

Kerreri
Omdurman · Halfiyeh
Khartoum

B.V. Parkinshire, Oxford.

CHAPTER 10

The Desert March of the Forlorn Hope

When years ago, I 'listed, lads.
To serve our Gracious Queen,
The sergeant made me understand
I was a 'Royal Marine.'
He said we sometimes served in ships,
And sometimes on the shore;
But did not say I should wear spurs,
Or be in the Camel Corps.
         Songs of the Camel Corps (Sergt. H. Eagle, R.M.C.C.)

Korti was a city of tents arrayed amid groves of fronded palm over-hanging the broad river; beyond, the illimitable coloured spaces of the desert, barred with plains of tawny grass set with mimosa, and green fields of *dhura*, and merging into the far rose-hued hills. All day long the strong sun smote upon its yellow avenues, and the bugles called, and the north wind, steady and cool, blew the boats up the river, and the men, ragged and cheery and tanned saddle-colour, came march-ing in and were absorbed into the great armed camp. Thence were to spring two long arms of fighting men, one to encircle the river, the other to reach across the desert, strike at Khartoum and save Gordon.

The day after I arrived at Korti, 5th January, 1885, the desert arm had bent back to obtain reinforcements; because there were not enough camels to furnish transport for the first march.

The first division of the Naval Brigade, under Lieutenant Alfred Pigott, also arrived on the 5th. Officers and men alike were covered with little black pustules, due to the poison carried by the flies. Nev-ertheless, they were fit and well and all *a-taunto*. They were brigaded under my command with Sir Herbert Stewart's Desert Column. The intention was that Gordon's steamers, then waiting for us somewhere between Metemmeh and Khartoum, should be manned with the sailors and a detachment of infantry, and should take Sir Charles Wilson up to Khartoum.

The second division of the Naval Brigade was still on its way up. It eventually joined us at Gubat. I may here say, for the sake of clearness, that Gubat is close to Metemmeh and that Shendi lies on the farther, or east, bank of the Nile, so that Gubat, Metemmeh and Shendi were really all within the area of the rendezvous at which the River Column under General Earle was intended to join forces with the Desert Column.

Sir Herbert Stewart arrived at Korti on the 5th and left that place on the 8th, the intervening days being occupied in preparations. An essential part of my own arrangements consisted in obtaining spare boiler-plates, rivets, oakum, lubricating oil, and engineers' stores generally, as I foresaw that these would be needed for the steamers, which had already been knocking about the Nile in a hostile country for some three months. At first, Sir Redvers Buller refused to let me have either the stores or the camels upon which to carry them. He was most good-natured and sympathetic, but he did not immediately perceive the necessity.

"What do you want boiler-plates for?" he said. "Are you going to mend the camels with them?"

But he let me have what I wanted. (I did mend the camels with oakum.) With other stores, I took eight boilerplates, and a quantity of rivets. One of those plates, and a couple of dozen of those rivets, saved the column.

The Gardner gun of the Naval Brigade was carried in pieces on four camels. Number one carried the barrels, number two training and elevating gear and wheels, number three the trail, number four, four boxes of hoppers. The limber was abolished for the sake of handiness. The gun was unloaded, mounted, feed-plate full, and ready to march in under four minutes. When marching with the gun, the men hauled it with drag-ropes, muzzle first, the trail being lifted and carried upon a light pole. Upon going into action, the trail was dropped and the gun was ready, all the confusion and delay caused by unlimbering in a crowded space being thus avoided.

At midday the 8th January, the Desert Column paraded for its second and final march, behind the village of Korti, and was inspected by

Lord Wolseley. The same thought inspired every officer and man: we are getting to the real business at last.

The Desert Column, quoting from the figures given in Sir Charles Wilson's excellent work, *From Korti to Khartoum*, was composed as follows:

	Officers	N.-C. Officers and Men
Staff	8	6
Naval Brigade	5	53
19th Hussars	9	121
Heavy Camel Regiment	24	376
M. I. Camel Regiment	21	336
Royal Artillery	4	39
Royal Sussex Regiment	16	401
Essex Regiment	3	55
Commissariat and Transport	5	72
Medical Staff		50
	98	1,509

And four guns (one Gardner, three 7-pr. screw guns), 304 natives, 2,228 camels, and 155 horses. Already there were along the route at the wells of Howeiyat (left on the first march), 33 officers and men of the M. I. Camel Regiment and 33 camels; and at Jakdul, 422 officers and men of the Guards' Camel Regiment (including Royal Marines), Royal Engineers, and Medical Staff, and 20 camels. The Desert Column picked up these detachments as it went along, leaving others in their places.

The column rode off at 2 o'clock p.m. amid a chorus of good wishes from our comrades. I rode my white donkey, County Waterford, which had been sent up to Korti by boat. We marched ten miles; halted at sunset and bivouacked, and started again half an hour after midnight. The moon rode high, and it was very cold; but the cold was invigorating; and the hard gravel or sand of the track made good going. Desert marching with camels demands perpetual attention; the loads slip on the camels and must be adjusted; a native driver unships the load and drops it to save himself trouble; camels stray or break loose. By means of perpetual driving, the unwieldy herd creeps forward with noiseless footsteps, at something under three miles an hour.

Although the camels were so numerous, their numbers had been

Mounted on board Ship.

General View of Naval Carriage for 5-Barrelled
Rifle-Calibre Gun.

reduced to the bare requirements of that small mobile column, which alone could hope to achieve the enterprise.

At 10 o'clock a.m. on the 9th, we halted for four hours in a valley of grass and mimosa trees; marched till sunset and came to another grassy valley and bivouacked. On the 10th we started before daylight, and reached the wells of El Howeiyat at noon, very thirsty, and drank muddy water and breakfasted; marched on until long after dark, over rough ground, the men very thirsty, the camels slipping and falling all over the place, and at length bivouacked. Starting again before daylight on the nth, we came to the wooded valley set among granite hills, where are the wells of Abu Haifa, men and animals suffering greatly from thirst. The wells consisted of a muddy pond and a few small pools of bitter water. More holes were dug, and the watering went on all the afternoon and all night.

Next morning, 12th January, we loaded up at daylight, and marched across the plain lying beneath the range of yellow hills, broken by black rocks, called Jebel Jelif; entered a grassy and wide valley, ending in a wall of rock; turned the corner of the wall, and came into a narrower valley, full of large round stones, and closed in at the upper end by precipices, riven into clefts, within which were the pools of Jakdul. We beheld roads cleared of stones, and the signboards of a camp, and the forts of the garrison, and stone walls crowning the hills, one high on the left, two high on the right hand.

In ten days, the little detachment of Guards, Royal Marines and Engineers under Major Dorward, R.E., had performed an incredible amount of work: road-making, wall-building, laying-out, canal-digging and reservoir-making. All was ready for Sir Herbert Stewart's force, which took up its quarters at once.

That evening the Guards gave an excellent dinner to the Staff, substituting fresh gazelle and sand-grouse for bullybeef. All night the men were drawing water from the upper pool of the wells, in which was the best water, by the light of lanterns.

The next day, 13th January, all were hard at work watering the camels and preparing for the advance on the morrow. The camels were already suffering severely: some thirty had dropped dead on the way; and owing to the impossibility of obtaining enough animals to carry the requisite grain, they were growing thin. It will be observed that the whole progress of the expedition depended upon camels as the sole means of transport.

When a camel falls from exhaustion, it rolls over upon its side, and

127

is unable to rise. But it is not going to die unless it stretches its head back; and it has still a store of latent energy; for a beast will seldom of its own accord go on to the last. It may sound cruel; but in that expedition it was a case of a man's life or a camel's suffering. When I came across a fallen camel, I had it hove upright with a gun-pole, loaded men upon it, and so got them over another thirty or forty miles.

By the exercise of care and forethought, I succeeded in bringing back from the expedition more camels, in the proportion of those in my control, than others, much to the interest of my old friend Sir Redvers Buller. He asked me how it was done; and I told him that I superintended the feeding of the camels myself. If a camel was exhausted, I treated it as I would treat a tired hunter, which, after a long day, refuses its food. I gave the exhausted camels food by handfuls, putting them upon a piece of cloth or canvas, instead of throwing the whole ration upon the ground at once.

Major Kitchener (now Lord Kitchener of Khartoum), who was dwelling in a cave in the hillside, reported that Khashm-el-Mus Bey, Malik (King) of the Shagiyeh tribe, was at Shendi with three of Gordon's steamers. (He was actually at Nasri Island.) Lieutenant E. J. Montagu-StuartWortley, King's Royal Rifles, joined the column for service with Sir Charles Wilson in Khartoum. Little did we anticipate in what his plucky service would consist. Colonel Burnaby came in with a supply of grain, most of which was left at Jakdul, as the camels which had brought it were needed to carry stores for the column. There were 800 Commissariat camels, carrying provisions for 1500 men for a month, the first instalment of the depot it was intended to form at Metemmeh, as the base camp from which to advance upon Khartoum.

With Burnaby came Captain Gascoigne, who had special knowledge of the Eastern Soudan, and who afterwards went up to Khartoum with Sir Charles Wilson.

The column left Jakdul at 2 o'clock p.m. on 14th January, and marched for three hours. It was generally supposed that we might be attacked between Jakdul and Metemmeh, a distance of between 70 and 80 miles; although the only intelligence we had was Major Kitchener's report that 3000 men under the *Mahdi's emir* were at Metemmeh. We did not know that the occupation of Jakdul by Sir Herbert Stewart on the 2nd of January, had moved the *Mahdi* to determine upon the destruction of the Desert Column between Jakdul and Metemmeh. The news of the occupation of Jakdul had travelled with extraordinary swiftness.

It was known on the 4th January, or two days after the event, in Berber, nearly 90 miles from Jakdul as the crow flies; and on that day the Emir of Berber dispatched his men to reinforce the Emir of Metemmeh. If the news were known in Berber and Metemmeh it must have run through the whole surrounding area of desert. The ten days occupied by the column in returning to Korti and returning again to Jakdul, gave the enemy the time they needed to concentrate in front of us. Moreover, Omdurman had fallen during the second week in January, setting free a number of the *Mahdi's* soldiers. But of these things we were ignorant when we pushed out of Jakdul. We picked up a Remington rifle, and saw some horse-tracks, and that was all.

During the second night out from Jakdul (the 15th-16th) the camels were knee-lashed and dispositions were made in case of attack, but nothing happened. It was the last night's rest we were to have for some time.

On the morning of the 16th, we started as usual in the dark. When the light came, we saw the hills of Abu Klea in the distance, and after marching nearly to them, halted for breakfast. In the meantime, Lieutenant-Colonel Barrow, with his squadron of the 19th Hussars, had gone ahead to occupy the wells of Abu Klea. About 11 a.m. Barrow returned to report that there was a large force of the enemy between us and the wells. The column was then lying in a shallow valley, whence the track led uphill over rough ground towards a pass cleft in the range of hills, beyond which were the wells.

The column fell in and mounted at once. Through glasses we could clearly distinguish innumerable whiterobed figures of Arabs, relieved upon the black cliffs dominating the pass, leaping and gesticulating. Here and there were puffs of smoke, followed after an interval by a faint report; but the range was too far, and no bullet arrived. Nearer hand, were swiftly jerking the isolated flags of the signallers, communicating from the advanced scouts to the main body. The Naval Brigade with the Mounted Infantry, which were on the left of the column, were ordered to ascend the hill on the left of the line of advance, to guard the flank of the column.

We dragged up the Gardner gun, placed it in position, and built a breastwork of loose stones. By the time we had finished, it was about 4 o'clock. Beyond and beneath us, a line of green and white flags was strung across the valley, fluttering above the scrub, and these, with a large tent, denoted the headquarters of the enemy.

The rest of the column were hurriedly building a *zeriba* in the valley. As the twilight fell, a party of the enemy crept to the summit of the hill on the right flank, opposite to our fort, and dropped bullets at long range into the column below, which replied with a couple of screw guns. As the darkness thickened, there arose that maddening noise of *tom-toms,* whose hollow and menacing beat, endlessly and pitilessly repeated, haunts those who have heard it to the last day of their lives. Swelling and falling, it sounds now hard at hand, and again far away. That night, we lay behind the breastwork, sleepless and very cold; and the deadly throbbing of the drums filled the air, mingled with the murmur of many voices and the rustle as of many feet, and punctuated with the sullen crack of rifles, now firing singly, now in a volley, and the whine of bullets. At intervals, thinking the enemy were upon us, we stood to arms.

When at last the day broke, there were thousands of white-robed figures clustering nearer upon the hills, and the bullets thickened, so that, chilled as we were, rather than attempt to warm ourselves by exercise we were fain to lie behind the breastwork. The Naval Brigade had no casualties.

Our detachment was speedily called in, so that we had no time for breakfast, which was being hastily eaten under fire by the rest of the column. All we had was a biscuit and a drink of water. We took up our position on the right front. Sir Herbert Stewart waited for a time in case the enemy should attack. Major Gough, commanding the Mounted Infantry, was knocked senseless by a bullet graze; Major Dickson of the Royals was shot through the knee; Lieutenant Lyall of the Royal Artillery was hit in the back.

Sir Herbert Stewart and Colonel Burnaby were riding about on high ground, a mark for the enemy. I saw the general's bugler drop close beside him, and running up, implored both him and Burnaby to dismount, but they would not. I had hardly returned to my place when I heard another bullet strike, and saw Burnaby's horse fall, throwing its rider. I went to help Burnaby to his feet, and as I picked him up, he said a curious thing. He said, "I'm not in luck today, Charlie."

When it became evident that the enemy would not attack, Sir Herbert Stewart decided to take the initiative. He ordered a square to be formed outside the *zeriba,* in which the baggage and the camels were to be left in charge of a small garrison.

In the centre of the square were to be camels, carrying water, ammunition, and *cacolets* (litters) for the wounded. I do not know how

HADENDOA WARRIOR

many camels there were. Count Gleichen says about 30; Colonel Colville, in the official history, gives the figure as 150. In the front of the square (looking from the rear of the square forward), left, and nearly all down the left flank, were Mounted Infantry; on the right front, and half-way down the right flank, Guards' Camel Regiment.

Beginning on the left flank where Mounted Infantry ended, and continuing round the rear face, were the Heavy Camel Regiment. Then, in the centre of the rear, was the Naval Brigade with Gardner gun. On the right of rear face, the Heavy Camel Regiment extended to the angle. Round the corner, lower right flank, were the Royal Sussex, then came the Royal Marines, continuing to the Guards' Camel Regiment. Behind the centre of the front ranks were the three screw guns. In case of attack, I was directed to use my own judgment as to placing the Gardner gun.

The square was thus formed under fire. Bear in mind that the column was upon the floor of a valley commanded by slopes and hill-tops occupied by the enemy. The route of the square lay over the lower slopes of the hills on the right, thus avoiding the hollow way on the left commanded by the enemy's breastworks. Captain Campbell's company of Mounted Infantry, and Colonel Barrow with his Hussars, went ahead to skirmish on the front and on the left flank, and somewhat checked the fire, while Lieutenant Romilly and a detachment of Scots Guards skirmished ahead on the right.

It was about 10 a.m. when the square began to move. The enemy, increasing their fire, kept pace with it. The route, studded with rocky knolls, furrowed with watercourses, and sharply rising and falling, was almost impassable for the camels. They lagged behind, slipping and falling, and we of the rear face were all tangled up with a grunting, squealing, reeking mass of struggling animals. Their drivers, terrified by the murderous fire coming from the right, were pressing back towards the left rear angle. By dint of the most splendid exertions, the sailors kept up, dragging the Gardner gun.

Men were dropping, and halts must be made while they were hoisted into the *cacolets* and their camels forced into the square. Surgeon J. Magill, attending a wounded skirmisher outside the square, was hit in the leg. During the halts the enemy's fire was returned, driving off large numbers on the hills to the right. In about an hour we covered two miles.

Then we saw, on the left front, about 600 yards away, a line of green and white flags twinkling on long poles planted in the grass and scrub. No one knew what these might portend. As the fire was hottest on the right, we thought that the main body would attack from that quarter. Suddenly, as we halted, more and yet more flags flashed above the green; and the next moment the valley was alive with black and white figures, and resounding with their cries. The whole body of them moved swiftly and in perfect order across our left front, disappearing behind rocks and herbage.

The square was instantly moved forward some thirty yards on the slope, in order to gain a better position. Ere the movement was completed, the enemy reappeared.

CHAPTER 11

The Fight at Abu Klea

England well may speak with wonder
Of the small heroic band,
Fearlessly, though parched and weary.
Toiling 'cross the desert sand;
How they met the foeman's onslaught,
Firm, undaunted, with a cheer,
Drove ten times or more their number,
Down the vale of Abu Klea.

> Songs of the Camel Corps (Serg. H. Eagle, R.M.C.C.)

Before the square was completely formed on the top of the knoll at the foot of which it had been halted when the thousands of Arabs sprang into view on the left front, the Arabs reappeared on the left rear, about 500 yards distant. They were formed into three phalanxes joined together, the points of the three wedges being headed by *emirs* or *sheikhs*, riding with banners. The horsemen came on at a hand-gallop, the masses of footmen keeping up with them. Our skirmishers were racing in for their lives. The last man was overtaken and speared.

At this moment the left rear angle of the square was still unformed. The camels were still struggling into it. Several camels, laden with wounded, had lain down at the foot of the slope and their drivers had fled into the square; and these animals were being dragged in by soldiers. The appalling danger of this open corner was instantly evident. I told the bugler to sound the halt, and having forced my way through the press to the front of the square, and reported the case to Sir Herbert Stewart, who said, "Quite right," I struggled back to the rear.

Then I ordered the crew of the Gardner gun to run it outside the square to the left flank. At the same time, Colonel Burnaby wheeled Number 3 Company (4th and 5th Dragoon Guards) from the rear face to the left flank. Number 4 Company (Scots Greys and Royals) had already wheeled from the rear to the left flank, so that they were just behind me. Five or six paces outside the square we dropped the trail of the gun. So swiftly did these things happen that the leading ranks of the enemy were still 400 yards away.

They were tearing down upon us with a roar like the roar of the sea, an immense surging wave of white-slashed black forms brandishing bright spears and long flashing swords; and all were chanting, as they leaped and ran, the war-song of their faith, "*La ilaha ill' Allah Mohammedu rasul Allah*"; and the terrible rain of bullets poured into them by the Mounted Infantry and the Guards stayed them not. They wore the loose white robe of the *Mahdi's* uniform, looped over the left shoulder, and the straw skullcap. These things we heard and saw in a flash, as the formidable wave swept steadily nearer.

I laid the Gardner gun myself to make sure. As I fired, I saw the enemy mown down in rows, dropping like ninepins; but as the men killed were in rear of the front rank, after firing about forty rounds (eight turns of the lever), I lowered the elevation. I was putting in most effective work on the leading ranks and had fired about thirty rounds when the gun jammed. The extraction had pulled the head from a discharged cartridge, leaving the empty cylinder in the barrel. William Rhodes, chief boatswain's mate, and myself immediately set to work to unscrew the feed-plate in order to clear the barrel or to take out its lock.

The next moment the enemy were on top of us. The feed-plate dropped on my head, knocking me under the gun and across its trail. Simultaneously a spear was thrust right through poor Rhodes, who was instantly killed at my side. Walter Miller the armourer was speared beside the gun at the same time. I was knocked off the trail of the gun by a blow with the handle of an axe, the blade of which missed me. An Arab thrust at me with his spear, and I caught the blade, cutting my hand, and before he could recover his weapon a bullet dropped him. Struggling to my feet, I was carried bodily backwards by the tremendous impact of the rush, right back upon the front rank of the men of Number 4 Company, who stood like rocks.

I can compare the press to nothing but the crush of a theatre crowd alarmed by a cry of fire. Immediately facing me was an Arab holding a spear over his head, the staff of the weapon being jammed against his back by the pressure behind him. I could draw neither sword nor pistol. The front ranks of our men could not use rifle or bayonet for

ABU-KLEA

a few moments. But the pressure, forcing our men backwards up the hill, presently enabled the rear rank, now occupying a position of a few inches higher than the enemy, to fire over the heads of the front rank right into the mass of the Arabs. The bullets whizzed close by my head; and one passed through my helmet. The Arabs fell in heaps, whereupon our front rank, the pressure upon them relaxing, fired, and fought hand to hand with the bayonet, cursing as the rifles jammed and the shoddy bayonets twisted like tin.

The enemy wavered and broke away, some retreating, but the greater number turning to the rear face of the square, carrying some of the Naval Brigade with them. The rest of my men manned the gun and opened fire on the retreating enemy. But by the time the gun was in action the retreating *dervishes* had hidden themselves in a *nullah*, and the main body of the enemy had burst into the gap left by the camels in the rear face. My men joined in the furious hand-to-hand fighting all among the jam of men and camels. The ranks of the front face of the square had turned about face and were firing inwards. Poor Burnaby (who was "not in luck today") was thrown from his horse, and was killed by a sword cut in the neck as he lay on the ground.

Fighting next to me in the square was "Bloody-minded Piggot"— Captain C. P. Piggot of the 21st Hussars—using a shot-gun charged with buck-shot. The Arabs were crawling and twisting under the camels and in and out the legs of the men, whom they tried to stab in the back, and Piggot was loading and firing, and the bluejackets kept calling to him, "Here's another joker, sir!" I saw the bald head of an Arab emerging from a pile of bodies, and as Piggot fired, I saw the bald crown riddled like the rose of a watering-pot.

One mounted *sheikh*, at least, won right into the square, where the bodies of himself and his horse were found afterwards.

Numbers 4 and 5 Company, who had withstood the first rush until they were pressed back upon the mass of camels, were still fighting in front when they were attacked in rear. There, the left wing of the Heavy Camel Regiment—Scots Greys, Royals, and 5th Dragoon Guards—did desperate hand-to-hand fighting in the square, while the right wing and the Royal Sussex by their steady fire kept off the rest of the enemy. The stress endured only a few minutes. Every Arab inside the square was slain. The camels, which had made the weak corner of the square, afterwards saved it by presenting a solid, irremovable obstacle to the enemy.

As the enemy retired, Sir Herbert Stewart gave the word, and our men cheered again and again, and the retreating Arabs turned and shook their fists at us.

Their desperate courage was marvellous. I saw a boy of some twelve years of age, who had been shot through the stomach, walk slowly up through a storm of bullets and thrust his spear at one of our men. I saw several Arabs writhe from out a pile of dead and wounded, and charge some eighty yards under fire towards us, and one of them ran right up to the bayonets and flung himself upon them and was killed. I saw an Arab, who was wounded in the legs, sit up, and hurl his spear at a passing soldier. As the soldier stopped to load his rifle, the Arab tried to reach another spear, and failing, caught up stones and cast them at his foe; and then, when the soldier presented his rifle and took a deliberate aim, the Arab sat perfectly still looking down the barrel, till the bullet killed him.

Surgeon-General Sir Arthur W. May tells me of an instance of the spirit of the men. A huge able seaman, nicknamed Jumbo, who was one of the gun's crew when it was run outside the square, was thrown upon his face by the charge; and apparently every Arab who went past or over him, had a dig at the prostrate seaman.

After the action, with the help of able seaman Laker, I carried him to the doctor. He was a mass of blood, which soaked my tunic. I tried to wash it afterwards with sand. He must have weighed about sixteen stone. Quite recently, at Stornoway, where he is chief petty officer of the Coastguard, I had the pleasure of meeting Mr. Laker, and we re-called the salving of poor Jumbo.

He had seventeen wounds, spear-thrusts, and sword-cuts. Upon visiting him in the Field Hospital a few days later, Surgeon May, in-tending to console the patient, said:

"You will be able to be sent back with the next convoy of wound-ed, after all."

"Sent back?" returned Jumbo indignantly. "I haven't done with the beggars yet!"

He recovered, but not in time to gratify his ardour.

The square was moved some 50 yards from the field of battle and was formed anew. I went to try to find any wounded men of my Brigade. Having brought in two, I was starting for a third time, when someone shouted, "Look out, Charlie!" and I turned about to see an Arab charging at me with a spear. I ran to meet him, sword in hand, parried his spear, then held my sword rigid at arm's length. He ran right up the blade to the hilt, against which his body struck with so

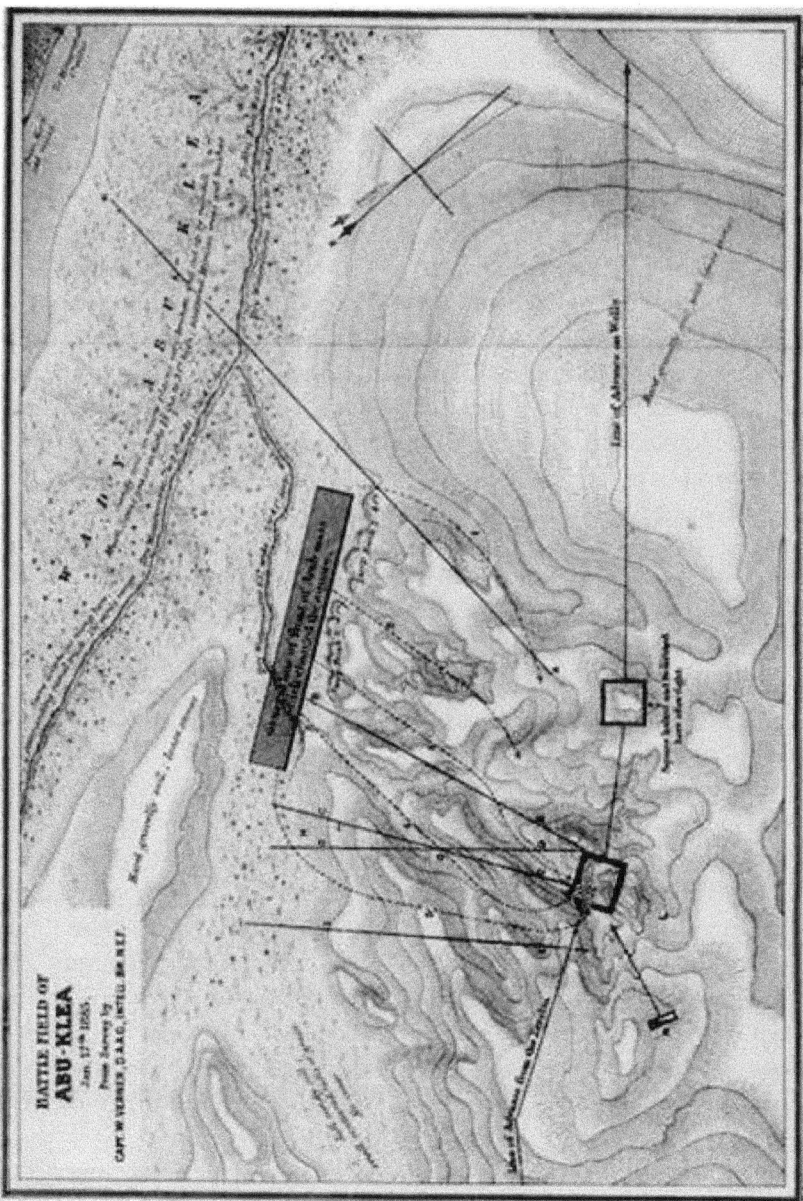

BATTLE FIELD OF
ABU-KLEA
Jan. 17th 1885.
From Survey by
CAPT. W. BERGE, D.A.Q. INTEL. BR. H.Q.

great force that he fell backward.

I picked up a man who was shot through the back, and put him upon a camel upon which was a wounded Arab. Presently I heard my man singing out; and I found his thumb was being chewed off by the Arab, whom I hauled off the camel and of whom I disposed in another way.

The bodies of most of my men who were killed were found some 25 yards from the place at which we had worked the gun. Here were the bodies of my poor comrades, Lieutenants Alfred Pigott and R. E. de Lisle. Pigott had been promoted to commander, but he never knew it. De Lisle had his whole face cut clean off. Captain C. P. Piggot (not to be confused with the naval officer, Commander Alfred Pigott), who fought like a Paladin in the square, and who knew not fear, died some years afterwards in England. (I took him on my coach to Lord's; he was so weak that he could not get upon it without the help of a footman, and he looked dreadfully ill. He told me that the doctor had given him three weeks to live; but he was dead in three days.)

Eight of the Naval Brigade were killed and seven were wounded, out of 40 who went into action. Every man of the brigade handling the gun outside the square was killed, excepting myself.

I observed that the rows of bullets from the Gardner gun, which was rifle calibre .45-inch, with five barrels, had cut off heads and tops of heads as though sliced horizontally with a knife.

The official account gives the loss of the enemy at 1,100 in the vicinity of the square.

Nearly half the British rifles jammed, owing to the use of leaf cartridges. The Remington rifles used by the *Mahdi's* soldiers had solid drawn cartridges which did not jam. During the action of Abu Klea, the officers were almost entirely employed in clearing jammed rifles passed back to them by the men. The British bayonets and cutlasses bent and twisted, the result of a combination of knavery and laziness on the part of those who were trusted to supply the soldier with weapons upon which his life depends. The bayonets were blunt, because no one had thought of sharpening them. The spears of the Arabs were sharp like razors. The cutlasses of the Naval Brigade were specially sharpened.

I noticed that when a soldier was killed, a bluejacket always endeavoured to secure his bayonet; and that when a sailor was killed, a soldier always tried to take his hat, preferring it to the army helmet.

The official report of Sir Charles Wilson states the total number of the enemy to have been from 9,000 to 11,000, consisting of men from Berber, Metemmeh, Kordofan, and 1,000 men of the *Mahdi's* army. Of the total number, it was estimated that 5,000 or 6,000 attacked. The British numbered something over 1,200 men; but these being in square, the weight of the attack fell upon no more than about 300 men. There were 342 men of the Royal Artillery on the front face of the square; 235 men on the left flank, reinforced when the charge came by some of the Naval Brigade and a company from the rear face; 300 men and the Naval Brigade, between 40 and 50 strong, on the rear face; and 307 men on the right flank.

The centre was a solid mass of camels. This thin framework of men, forced back upon the camels, resisted the tremendous impact of thousands of frenzied fanatics who knew not fear, and whom nothing stopped but death.

I cannot better describe the result than by quoting the words of Colonel the Hon. Reginald Talbot, 1st Life Guards, who commanded the Heavy Camel Regiment at Abu Klea (*Nineteenth Century*, Jan. 1886):

> It was an Inkerman on a small scale—a soldiers' battle; strength, determination, steadiness, and unflinching courage alone could have stemmed the onslaught.

It was a soldiers' battle, because the attack was sudden; it came before the square was formed; and in the stress and tumult orders were useless.

CHAPTER 12

The Fight to Reach the River

We had beat the foe at Abu Klea, and now had marched all night,
Parching with thirst, each longed to see the first faint streak of light,
For all expected with the dawn to see the river flow.
'Twas there all right, but in our path stood thousands of the foe;
We halted, and a barricade of biscuit boxes made,
And swift their deadly bullets flew round that frail barricade,
And many a gallant fellow dropped before the welcome cry,
'Form square' was heard, 'we must advance, and reach the Nile or die.'
                    Songs of the Camel Corps (Serg. H. Eagle, R.M.C.C.)

By the time the wounded were picked up, the dead counted, and their weapons destroyed, and the square was ready to start, it was half-past three in the afternoon. There was no food, and hardly any water. The soldiers suffered dreadfully from thirst; their tongues were so swollen as to cause intense pain, their lips black, their mouths covered with white mucus. Several men fainted. Luckily, I had put a skin of water upon a camel just before the action, so that the men of the Naval Brigade all had a drink, and there was a little water over for the wounded. The sailors persisted in smoking; they said it did them good; so, I let them.

The wells of Abu Klea lay some three miles ahead. The cavalry, the horses weak, emaciated, and tormented by thirst, were sent on to reconnoitre. The square followed slowly. So short-handed was the Naval Brigade that I had to clap on to the drag-ropes myself. We hauled the gun through the sand, and across *nullahs* and over rocks till about 5.30 p.m., when we came to the wells, which were small pools in the soil, and which, when they were emptied, slowly filled again. The water was yellow and of the consistency of cream; but it was cool, sweet, and delicious.

Three hundred volunteers from the Heavy Camel Regiment, the Guards' Camel Regiment, and the Mounted Infantry left the wells soon after sunset to march the six weary miles back again to fetch the camels and commissariat. They marched and worked all night; yet their lot was better than ours; for they got food and could keep warm. As for ourselves, we lay down where we were, without food or blankets, and suffered the coldest night in my remembrance.

It is suggested to me by a friend who has seen much active service in many wars, that, owing probably to the exhaustion of the nerves, men are far more susceptible to cold after a battle. He himself recalls the night after Magersfontein as the coldest he ever experienced. At any rate, we were cold to the marrow that night of 17th-18th January; cold and bruised and very hungry, the most of us having had no food for twenty-four hours. I must here record my admiration of the medical staff, who worked hard all night, doing their utmost for the sick and wounded.

I sat on an ammunition box and shivered. The wound upon my finger, where the Arab's spear had cut it, though slight, was disproportionately painful. Lieutenant Douglas Dawson (of the Coldstream Guards) came to me and asked me if I had any tobacco, I told him that my tobacco, together with my field-glasses, had departed into the desert with my steed *County Waterford*, which had run away. Dawson had six cigarettes, of which he gave me three. I would cheerfully have given a year's income for them, as I told him. We agreed that it was hard to have to die without knowing who had won the Derby.

At about seven o'clock next morning (18th January) the convoy returned with the rest of the camels and the commissariat. We had our first meal for some thirty-six hours. Then we went to work to build a fort in which to leave the wounded, and to prepare for the march to the river, some 25 miles distant. A burying party went back to the field of Abu Klea and interred our dead. Some prisoners captured by the convoy on its way back to the camp, reported that Omdurman had fallen; but the information was not made generally known. I did not hear it until we reached Metemmeh.

Sir Herbert Stewart then determined to reach the Nile before next morning. A small detachment of the Royal Sussex was left to guard the wounded. The column marched about 3.30 p.m. It was a desperate venture, for the men had had no sleep for two nights, had fought a battle in between, had suffered agonies of thirst and the exhaustion of hunger. But Sir Herbert Stewart had learned from the prisoners that the enemy who had fought at Abu Klea were no more than the advanced guard of the main body, which would probably come out from Metemmeh to meet us, and that the fall of Omdurman had released a number of the *Mahdi's* army; and the general wished to reach the river before fighting again. He hoped to be upon the Nile before daylight. In any event, the enterprise of the Desert Column was a forlorn hope; and by this time, we all knew it.

Cameron, war correspondent of *The Standard*, came to me with a very grave face. He was not alarmed for his own safety, for he was a most gallant man; but he feared for the column.

"Lord Charles," he said, "have you any influence with General Stewart? If so, for God's sake implore him not to go on without reinforcements. I know these people and he does not."

The next time I saw poor Cameron was upon the following day, when he was lying with a bullet-hole in his forehead, dead.

The column was guided by Ali Loda, a friendly desert freebooter who had been captured during the first march to Jakdul. He was accompanied by Captain Verner and Colonel Barrow. Half the force marched on foot, in case of attack; the mounted men each leading a camel. The commissariat camels were tied in threes, nose to tail, the leading camel being ridden by a native driver. Although both men and camels were tired out, they went bravely along the track leading across a wide plain, with grass and scrub in the distance. By the time it was dark, we had come to the long *savas* grass, and the tracks, hitherto plain to see in the brilliant starlight, became obscured.

Then began the confusion. By this time men and camels were utterly exhausted. There was no moon, but no lights were allowed, and all orders were to be given in a whisper. The camels, weary and famished, lagged and tumbled down; their riders went to sleep and fell off; the leading camels fell behind; and the rear camels, most of them riderless, straggled up to the front. The formation was totally disordered. In the darkness the confusion speedily became inextricable. When there was a halt to wait for stragglers, the men lay down and dropped asleep. About this time the column blundered into a wood of acacia trees armed with long sharp thorns. There ought to have been no such wood; indeed, Count Gleichen avers that no one ever found it afterwards.

In this state of affairs, the column lost in the dark in an unknown country, utterly worn out, and inextricably tangled upon itself, I made the Naval Brigade unspan and gave them tea, then we struggled on,

Sudanese warriors

hour after hour. As for silence, the noise might have been heard and probably was heard at Metemmeh. An immense multitudinous murmur went up from the unhappy mob of swearing men and roaring, squealing, grumbling camels. A longer or more exhausting nightmare I never suffered.

Daylight came at last. It was about 6 o'clock on the morning of 19th January. The least we had hoped was to have come within sight of the Nile. But when the column halted there was no Nile; only a long gravel slope rising before us, set with scattered trees rising from the eternal *Savas* grass and low scrub. Captain Verner went ahead to reconnoitre, and the column toiled on up the ridge. Then, at last, upon reaching the top at about 7 o'clock, we beheld the wide valley, and the Nile flowing between broad belts of green, and on the left, the roofs of a chain of villages, and the walled town of Metemmeh.

Beyond, upon the farther bank, clustered the huts of the village of Shendi. But we had not yet come to the river. And moving out from Metemmeh were crowds of the enemy, moving out to cut us off from the blessed water. Once more, the whole air was throbbed with the boding war-drums.

Sir Herbert Stewart determined to give the men breakfast and then to attack. As usual, a *zeriba* must first be constructed and the force put in *laager*. The column was halted upon the top of the rising ground, in a space some 300 yards square, surrounded by a sea of thin scrub, in which the enemy could find cover. A parapet, square in plan, and about two feet six inches high, was constructed of saddles and biscuit boxes and anything else which would serve the purpose. The camels were pushed inside it, and knee-lashed, and in the centre was placed the hospital. During the progress of the work the enemy, concealed in the scrub, crept nearer and opened fire.

The men breakfasted in a rain of bullets. So wearied were they, that some fell asleep over their food, bullets singing all about them. Many of the men got no food at all. I saw two men shot while they slept. One *dervish* in particular sniped the Naval Brigade all breakfast-time. I subsequently discovered him in the bush, lying dead, a bullet through his head, in a litter of about 200 spent cartridges. One of my men was shot, and a spoke was knocked out of the wheel of the Gardner gun. A soldier was shot through the stomach, and was carried screaming to the doctors, who gave him *laudanum*.

The situation was far from encouraging. During the night—the third without sleep—the men had marched for 14 hours, covering 19 miles, and losing some hundred camels. We were still four miles from the river, and between the river and our exhausted force were thousands of raging *dervishes*. We were caught in a trap.

Seventy yards from our left flank was a little hill. In order to prevent its capture by the enemy, 30 Guardsmen were told off to occupy it. Volunteers carried saddles and boxes across the bullet-swept space and built a small breastwork with them. Several men were knocked over. In the meantime, a company was extended along the ridge some 50 yards beyond the *zeriba* to check the enemy's fire; but they had nothing at which to aim except the puffs of smoke rising above the scrub, The Naval Brigade had no better luck with the Gardner gun, placed outside the *zeriba* near the left angle of the front.

At some time between 9 and 10 o'clock Sir Herbert Stewart was hit in the groin and severely wounded. The knowledge of this disaster was concealed from the men as long as possible. Then followed a terrible interval, which lasted for hours. Under that pitiless fire, exposed to an invisible enemy, men and camels were being hit every minute. All this time the heat was intense. There we lay in the blazing sun, helpless, the rattle of rifles all around us, the thin high note of the bullets singing overheard, or ending with a thud close at hand; men crying out suddenly, or groaning; camels lying motionless and silent, blood trickling from their wounds; and no one seemed to know what we were going to do. Of all things, the most trying to a soldier is to lie still under fire without being able to reply. It is true that there was volley firing in reply to the enemy, but they were invisible,

The command had naturally devolved upon Colonel Sir Charles Wilson, R.E., head of the Intelligence Department. It was clear to me that unless we marched against the enemy at once, we were done. I dispatched a written message to Sir Charles Wilson. The messenger was killed. I sent a second message by Sub-Lieutenant E. L. Munro, R.N., who was struck by a bullet which wounded him in seven places.

Shortly afterwards I received a message from Sir Charles Wilson informing me that he was about to march against the enemy. I was ordered to remain in command of the *zeriba*, with Colonel Barrow.

Before forming square, Sir Charles Wilson ordered the breastwork surrounding the hospital and that defending the little knoll occupied by the Guards in our rear, to be strengthened into redoubts, in case of attack. The ammunition boxes must be shifted from the inside of the main *zeriba*, and carried across and among the baggage and the packed and helpless camels, a slow, laborious and dangerous business performed under fire. Men and officers worked with a will; yet it was 2 o'clock in the afternoon before they had done. Just then St. Leger Herbert, private secretary to Sir Herbert Stewart and correspondent of *The Morning Post*, was shot through the head.

The square was composed of half the Heavy Camel Regiment, Guards, Mounted Infantry, Royal Sussex, Royal Engineers, and some dismounted Hussars. Sir Charles Wilson placed it under the executive command of Lieutenant-Colonel the Hon. E. E. Boscawen. The square was formed up in rear of the *zeriba* at 2.30 and marched at 3 o'clock. The men were cool, alert, and perfectly determined. The British soldier had shut his mouth. He was going to get to the river, enemy or no enemy, or die. By this time the enemy were plainly visible in full force in front, horse and foot gathering behind a line of green and white banners.

The moment the square moved beyond the redoubt, it received a heavy fire. Several men were hit, and were carried back to the *zeriba* by our men, while the square moved forward at quick march. It made a zigzag course in order to take advantage of the clear patches of ground among the scrub; lying down and firing, and again advancing.

The Naval Brigade mounted the Gardner gun in the angle of the redoubt, and, together with the Royal Artillery and two of their screw-guns under Captain Norton, maintained a steady fire at the three distinct masses of the enemy. Two of these were hovering in front of the advancing square, upon the landward slope of the hill rising between us and the river; the third threatened the *zeriba*. In all of these we dropped shells, paying particular attention to the body menacing the *zeriba*. When the shells burst in their midst, the *dervishes* scattered like a flock of starlings.

In the *zeriba* were the most of the Hussars, whose horses were worn out, the Royal Artillery, half the Heavy Camel Regiment, half the Royal Engineers, what was left of the Naval Brigade, and the wounded in the hospital. Some 2000 camels were knee-lashed outside and all round the larger *zeriba*, forming a valuable breastwork.

All we could do was to work our guns. As the square went on, the enemy, moving in large masses, shifted their position, and as they moved, we dropped shells among them, We judged their numbers to be greater than at Abu Klea. Would the square of only 900 men ever get through? If ever a little British Army looked like walking to certain death, it was that thin square of infantry.

Presently it disappeared from view. Soon afterwards we heard the steady roll of volley firing, and we knew that the enemy were charging the square. Then, silence. Whether the enemy had been driven back, or the square annihilated, we did not know. What we did know was that if the square had been defeated, the *zeriba* would very soon be attacked in overwhelming force. But as the moments passed the strain of suspense slackened; for, as the fire of the enemy directed upon the *zeriba* diminished and soon ceased altogether, the presumption was that the square had been victorious and had got through to the river.

What had happened was that the Arabs, charging downhill at the left front angle of the square, had been met by concentrated rifle fire, our men aiming low at a range of 400 yards, steady as on parade. Once more the British soldier proved that no troops in the world can face his musketry. The front ranks of the charging thousands were lying dead in heaps; the rear ranks fled over the hills; and the square went on, unmolested, very slowly, because the men were tired out, and so came to the river.

Count Gleichen, who marched with the square, recounting his experiences (*With the Camel Corps up the Nile*), writes:

Soon in the growing dusk a silver streak was visible here and there in amongst the green belt, but it was still a couple of miles off.... Our pace could not exceed a slow march. The sun went down, and the twilight became almost darkness; ... a two-days-old crescent was shining in the sky, and its feeble light guided us through the gravel hills right to the brink of the Nile. The men were as wild with joy as their exhausted condition would allow. The wounded were held up for one look at the gleaming river, and then hurried to the banks. Still, perfect discipline was observed. Not a man left his place in the ranks until his company was marched up to take its fill.... A chain of sentries was established on the slopes overlooking the square, and in two minutes the force was fast asleep.

Sir Charles Wilson (*From Korti to Khartoum*) adds:

The men were so exhausted that when they came up from their drink at the river they fell down like logs.

They had been marching and fighting for four days and three nights without sleep, and with very little food and water, and had lost a tenth of their number. That night we in the *zeriba* also slept. I remember very little about it, except that Lieutenant Charles Crutchley,

Adjutant of the Guards' Camel Regiment, woke me twice and asked me for water. He made no complaint of any kind, and I did not know that he had been hit early in the day and that he had a bullet in his leg. General Crutchley, who was so kind as to write to me in reply to my request that he would tell me what he remembers of the affair, says:

> I remember lying on a stretcher that night, and people knocking against my leg, and that my revolver was stolen, I believe by one of the camel boys.

Crutchley was carried down to the river by my bluejackets next day, and was taken into hospital. As I remember the occasion, he left the decision as to whether or not his leg should be amputated, to me. At any rate, the surgeon had no doubt as to the necessity of the operation, at which I was present. With his finger he flicked out of the wound pieces of bone like splinters of bamboo. The leg was buried, and was afterwards exhumed in order to extract the bullet from it. I think I remember that Crutchley, seeing it being carried across to the hospital, asked whose leg it was. He was carried upon a litter back to Korti, and the shaking of that terrible march made necessary a second operation, which was successful.

Sir Charles Wilson's force, having bivouacked that night beside the Nile, were up at daybreak; took possession of the empty village of mud huts, called Abu Kru, but always known as Gubat, which stood on the gravel ridge sloping to the Nile, 780 yards from the river; and placed the wounded in Gubat under a guard, The force then returned to our *zeriba*.

When we saw that gallant little array come marching over the distant hill-top, and through the scrub towards us, we cheered again and again. Hearty were our greetings. Our comrades, who had marched without breakfast, were speedily provided with a plentiful meal of bully-beef and tea.

Then we all set to work to dismantle the *zeriba*, to collect the stores of which it was constructed and to sort them out, to mend the broken saddles, and load up the wretched camels, who had been knee-lashed and unable to move for twenty-four hours. About a hundred camels were dead, having been shot as they lay. As there were not enough camels to carry all the stores, a part of these were left under an increased garrison inside the redoubt upon the knoll in rear of the *zeriba*, Major T. Davison in command.

At midday we buried the dead, over whom I read the service, Sir

Charles Wilson being present as chief mourner.

The last of the wounded to be moved was Sir Herbert Stewart, so that he should be spared as much discomfort as possible. He was doing fairly well, and we then hoped that he would recover.

Before sunset we were all safely lodged in Gubat. The Desert Column had reached the river at last. It was the 20th January; we had left Korti on the 8th. In the course of that 176 miles, we had gone through perhaps as sharp a trial as British troops have endured.

At the fight of Abu Klea, nine officers and 65 non-commissioned officers and men were killed, and nine officers and 85 non-commissioned officers and men were wounded, On the 19th January, between the wells of Abu Klea and the river, one officer and 22 non-commissioned officers and men were killed, and eight officers and 90 non-commissioned officers and men were wounded. The general, Sir Herbert Stewart, had received a wound which was to prove mortal. All the officers of the Naval Brigade, except Mr. James Webber, boatswain, and Sub-Lieutenant Munro, who was wounded, and myself, had been killed.

The losses were roughly one-tenth of the total number of the column. The camels which survived had been on one-third rations and without water for a week. They were hardly able to walk; ulcerating sores pitted their bodies; their ribs actually came through their skin. Count Gleichen says that his camel drank from the Nile for 14 minutes without stopping; and that subsequently the poor beast's ribs took a fine polish from the rubbing of the saddle. The horses of the hussars had been 58 hours, and many of them 72 hours, without water. I cannot mention the hussars without paying a tribute to the admirable scouting work they did under Lieutenant-Colonel Barrow during the whole march, up to the time the last *zeriba* was formed, when the gallant little horses were dead beat. The present field-marshal, Sir John French, did splendid service with the hussars throughout the campaign.

When we came into Gubat I was painfully, though not seriously, ill. The galling of the makeshift saddle during my three days' ride across the desert from Dal to Abu Fatmeh on my way to Korti, had developed into a horrid carbuncle; and I was unable to walk without help.

CHAPTER 13

Disaster

Comrades, who with us side by side,
Did in the brunt of battle stand,
Are absent now, their manly forms
Lie mouldering in the desert sand.
          Songs of the Camel Corps (Serg. H. Eagle, R.M.C.C.)

On 21st January, the day after the main body of the Desert Column had come to Gubat, an attack was made upon Metemmeh, which resolved itself into a reconnaissance in force. Lord Wolseley's instructions to Sir Herbert Stewart were "to advance on Metemmeh, which you will attack and occupy." These instructions Sir Charles Wilson, upon whom the command had devolved, determined to carry into execution, although there was a doubt whether under the circumstances the attempt would be justified. Metemmeh was a walled town of considerable strength, lying two miles down the river from the encampment. Between the encampment and the town rose low ridges, in whose folds clustered the huts of deserted villages.

The Naval Brigade joined in the attack; and as I was out of action, Mr. Webber, boatswain, was in command, and did admirably well.

While Sir Charles Wilson's force was firing upon the town, whence the enemy briskly replied, Gordon's four steamers arrived. His local troops instantly landed with guns, and joyfully bombarded the mud walls; while Sir Charles Wilson conferred with Khashm-el-Mus Bey, Malik (King) of the Shagiyeh tribe, and Abd-el-Hamid Bey, a young Arab greatly trusted by Gordon, who were in command of the steamers. Abd el Hamid subsequently deserted, and was, I think, shot by the *Mahdi*. Khashm-el-Mus having reported that a large force was on its way down from Khartoum under Feki Mustapha, Sir Charles Wilson decided that he ought not to incur the further loss of men involved in the capture of Metemmeh. He therefore withdrew from Metemmeh, and returned to Gubat, destroying the three intervening villages on the way.

During the reconnaissance of Metemmeh, Major William H. Poë, of the Royal Marines, was severely wounded in the leg. He insisted upon wearing a red coat, saying that his other coat was not fit to be seen; and he made a conspicuous target. His leg was amputated, and he eventually recovered; and he rides to hounds to this day.

In view of the approach of the enemy, the wounded were brought from the fort on the ridge to an entrenched camp on the river; and opposite to it, upon Gubat Island, a breastwork was constructed, and was occupied by some of Gordon's Soudanese who had come in the steamers. Major T. Davison's outlying detachment, with the remaining stores, was brought in.

It was now necessary very carefully to consider the situation. Sir Charles Wilson read the letters dispatched by Gordon and brought in one of the steamers, the *Bordein*, which had left Khartoum on 14th December. Sir Charles gave me these letters to read. In a letter addressed to the Officer Commanding H.M. Troops, Gordon requested that "all Egyptian officers and soldiers" be taken out of the steamer. He wrote:

> I make you a present of these *hens*, and I request you will not let one come back here to me.

In another letter, addressed to Major Watson (colonel in the Egyptian Army), dated 14th December, Gordon wrote that he expected a crisis to arrive about Christmas; and implied that he had abandoned hope of relief.

It was now nearly a month after Christmas, and Khartoum was still holding out. But it was no longer possible to carry into execution Lord Wolseley's original intention: that Sir Herbert Stewart should capture and occupy Metemmeh; that I should man Gordon's four steamers with the Naval Brigade and should take Sir Charles Wilson with a detachment of infantry up to Khartoum. Now, Sir Herbert Stewart was incapacitated by his wound; it was not considered practicable to take Metemmeh; all the officers of the Naval Brigade were killed or wounded except Mr. Webber; and I myself was so ill as to be unable to get about without help. Moreover, the weakened Desert Column, including more than a hundred wounded, would in all likelihood shortly be attacked by a greatly superior force.

Two main provisions of the original plan, however, had been fulfilled. The column had reached the river; and Gordon's steamers had joined the column. And it was then supposed that Wolseley was marching across the Bayuda Desert with reinforcements.

Sir Charles Wilson determined to go to Khartoum (a decision in which I strongly supported him), provided that he could make reasonably sure that the force to be left behind was not in immediate danger of attack. He reckoned that the news of the defeat of the *Mahdi's* forces at Abu Klea would have served both to inspirit the garrison at Khartoum, and, owing to the dispatch of a number of the enemy to meet us, to relieve them in some measure. And after examining the commanders of the steamers on the point, he was satisfied that the delay of two days spent in reconnoitring, would not be material; a conclusion which was not shared by Khashm-el-Mus, who was eager to go to Khartoum,

Accordingly, on 22nd January, Sir Charles Wilson took three steamers downstream to reconnoitre. The four boats sent down by Gordon were: the *Bordein*, under Abd-el-Hamid; *Talahawiyeh*, under Nusri Pasha; *Safieh*, under Mahmoud Bey; and *Tewfikiyeh*, under Khashm-el-Mus. Sir Herbert Stewart was moved on board the *Tewfikiyeh*, a small boat, which was employed as a ferry between Gubat Island and the mainland. I went with Sir Charles Wilson in the *Talahawiyeh*. I was not of much use, as I had to be helped on board, and was obliged to lie down in the cabin. In the same steamer were Major Phipps and two companies of Mounted Infantry. Old Khashm-el-Mus was made commandant of the boat instead of Nusri Pasha. In the *Bordein* were Captain Verner, Abd-el-Hamid, and native soldiers. The *Safieh* had her own crew and captain.

These vessels, about the size and build of the old penny steamboats on the Thames, had been ingeniously protected and armed by poor Colonel Stewart, he who was treacherously murdered on 18th September, 1884, after the wreck of his steamer *Abbas* at Hebbeh. (It will be remembered that Colonel Stewart was sent by Gordon, with a party of refugees, to communicate in person with the authorities in Egypt.) In the bows was a small turret constructed of baulks of timber, and containing a 9-pr. brass howitzer (*canon rayé*) to fire ahead; amidships, between the paddle-boxes, was the central turret, also built of timber, and mounting a gun to fire over the paddle-boxes.

Astern, on the roof of the deckhouse, was an enclosure of boiler-plate, protecting the wheel and giving shelter to riflemen. The sides and bulwarks were covered with boiler-plate, above which was fixed a rail of thick timber, leaving a space through which to fire. The boiler, which projected above the deck, was jacketed with logs of wood. The improvised armour of wood and iron would stop a bullet, but was pervious by shell.

The ships' companies were an interesting example of river piracy. The steamers had been cruising up and down the Nile since October, a period of four months, during which the crews lived on the country, raiding and fighting. Everything was filthy and neglected except the engines. The forehold was crammed with ammunition, *dhura* grain, wool, fuel, and miscellaneous loot. The main-hold was inhabited by women, babies, stowaways, wounded men, goats, amid a confusion of ammunition, sacks of grain, wood fuel, bedding and loot. The after-hold held the possessions, including loot, of the commandant. Below the forward turret slave-girls ceased not from cooking *dhura*-cakes. Rats swarmed everywhere; the whole ship exhaled a most appalling stench; and the ship's company shouted and screamed all day long.

First there was the commandant, who was theoretically in chief command of the ship, and who commanded the soldiers on shore; then there was the officer commanding the regular soldiers, Souda-nese. He was black, and so were his men, who were freed slaves. The officer commanding the artillery was an Egyptian. The *bashi-bazouk* contingent was composed of Shagiyehs—who were of the tribe ruled by Khashm-el-Mus—of black slaves, and of half-castes. Their officers were Turks, Kurds, and Circassians. The captain of the ship was a Don-golese, and his sailors were blacks. Under the captain were numerous petty officers, such as the chief of the sailors, the chief of the carpen-ters, and so forth. The chief engineer and his staff were Egyptians. The *reis* (pilot) and his assistants were Dongolese.

Into this wild medley, in the *Talahawiyeh*, Sir Charles Wilson brought a company of Mounted Infantry; and thus reinforced, we steamed down river; while I lay in the cabin, in a good deal of pain, and chatted to Khashm-el-Mus, who became a great friend of mine. He was a short, grey-bearded, dignified man of middle age, owning great power over his own people. He remained loyal to Gordon under very trying conditions, and he stuck by us to the last.

Near Shendi, one of Khashm-el-Mus's men came on board and reported that the force advancing from Berber had met the fugitives from Abu Klea and had come no farther. Another Shagiyeh gave the same information. The people of Shendi fired on the steamers, which replied with ten rounds of shell from each gun. We then went about and returned to Gubat. At my request, Sir Charles Wilson conferred upon Mr. Ingram, of *The Illustrated London News*, the rank of acting-lieutenant in the Royal Navy. Ingram had been of the greatest service. He had brought his own launch up from Korti, volunteered to the Desert Column, and fought gallantly at Abu Klea and at the reconnaissance of Metemmeh. As all the naval officers had been killed or wounded, and I was comparatively helpless, I was delighted to secure Mr. Ingram, who was exceedingly useful,

His subsequent history was remarkable. He was killed while hunting big game in Africa, and was buried upon an island, which was afterwards washed away. The story goes that the manner of his death and the bearing away by a flood of his remains, were the fulfilment of a curse, which fell upon him when, in spite of warnings, he purchased a certain Egyptian mummy.

Sir Charles Wilson, being assured that no attack was intended from the direction of Berber, began immediately to prepare for his expedition to Khartoum. Most unfortunately, I was compelled to retire into hospital; but I was able to issue instructions which I hope were of use. At Sir Charles Wilson's request, I advised him to take the two larger and better protected steamers, *Bordein* and *Talahawiyeh*.

The work of preparing them began next morning, 23rd January. The first thing to be done was to sort out from their crews the Egyptians, Turks, Kurds, Circassians, the "hens" whom Gordon had refused to have again in Khartoum, and to man the two vessels with Soudanese sailors and soldiers. Captain Gascoigne and Lieutenant Stuart-Wortley toiled at this tiresome job nearly all day.

At my suggestion, the people removed from the steamers were placed in a camp by themselves up stream, on the Khartoum side of Gubat; so that in the event of a force advancing from Khartoum, and the consequent revolt of the "hens," we should not be placed between two fires. The military objection was that they would foul the water; which was obviated by my building wooden piers projecting into the stream.

An engine-room artificer from the Naval Brigade was sent on board each steamer, in which they went to work to repair defects. Wood for the steamers was obtained by cutting up the *sakiehs*, or water-wheels, up and down the river, a slow process as performed by natives receiving orders through interpreters. Khashm-el-Mus was placed in command of the *Bordein*, and Abd-el-Hamid of the *Tala-*

hawiyeh. Sir Charles Wilson was to go in the *Bordein*, together with Captain Gascoigne, 10 non-commissioned officers and men of the Royal Sussex, one petty officer and one artificer

Naval Brigade, and 110 Soudanese soldiers. In the *Talahawiyeh* were Captain L. J. Trafford, in command of 10 non-commissioned officers and men of the Royal Sussex, one of whom was a signaller, one engine-room artificer Naval Brigade, and some 80 Soudanese soldiers. The *Talahawiyeh* towed a *nuggar* carrying about 50 Soudanese soldiers and a cargo of grain for Khartoum. According to Gordon's express desire, the British troops were clad in red tunics, which, being borrowed from the Guards and the Heavy Camel Regiment, were far from being a regimental fit.

By the time the preparations were complete, it was too late to start that night, and the Royal Sussex, folded in their red tunics, bivouacked on the bank.

During the day, the entrenchments upon the hillside and by the river were strengthened; and the same evening a convoy and an escort under the command of Colonel Talbot started for Jakdul to fetch stores. Captain C. B. Piggot, the man who knew not fear, carrying dispatches to Korti, accompanied them.

It should be borne in mind that the chief object of the expedition to Khartoum, apart from the necessity of communicating with Gordon himself, was to produce a moral effect upon the *Mahdists*; Gordon's idea being that the presence of a small force of British soldiers would inevitably convince the native that powerful reinforcements might be expected immediately. In the *journal* of Sir Charles Wilson (*From Korti to Khartoum*) he makes the following comment:

> The original plan was for Beresford to man two of the steamers with the Naval Brigade, mount his Gardner gun on one of them, and after overhauling them, take me to Khartoum with about fifty men of the Sussex Regiment. This was now impossible: all the naval officers were killed or wounded except Beresford, who was himself unable to walk, and many of the best petty officers and seamen were also gone. Beresford offered to accompany me; but he had done himself no good by going down the river the day before, and there was every prospect of his getting worse before he was better. Besides, I felt I could not deprive the force of its only naval officer, when it was quite possible the steamers left behind might have to take part in a fight.

That possibility was fulfilled. In the event, if I may say so, it was lucky that I was there.

At eight o'clock on the morning of the 24th January, the two steamers started, flying the Egyptian flag, the slave-girls frying *dhura*-cake under the fore turret, old Khashm-el-Mus smoking and drinking coffee on the cabin sofa, both vessels crammed with yelling and joyous savages, among whom were a bare score of British soldiers. They must pass powerful batteries, a single shot from which would sink them, and dangerous cataracts sown with rocks, and finally the guns of Omdurman, which was now in possession of the enemy. And having survived these perils, they might be unable to return, for the river was rapidly falling. Slowly they steamed away against the strong stream, and vanished; and for seven days we waited for news of that desperate enterprise.

In Sir Charles Wilson's absence, the military command devolved upon Colonel Boscawen, and after a few days, Colonel Boscawen being ill with fever, upon Colonel Mildmay Willson of the Scots Guards. The actual senior officer was myself. I issued a proclamation to the natives.

(Translation)

To the people of the river districts.

This is to make it known to you that we are the advanced portion of the two great English Armies which are now marching on Khartoum to punish the rebels.

We do not wish to do you any harm if you will come to see us. You will receive no hurt; and we will pay you for your cattle and crops.

If, however, you do not tender your submission, we will punish you severely. Your cattle will be taken, your villages and *sakiehs* burnt, and you yourselves will be killed, even as those unfortunates who ventured to oppose us at Abu Klea and Metemmeh. Any person desirous of speaking with the English general should carry a white flag, and come by the river bank alone. He will not be detained, and he will be guarded from all danger.

The *Sirdar*
Advanced Guard, English Army

I was in hospital for only two days. The surgeon's knife relieved my pain, and I was speedily healed. On the 26th January, and the following day, I took the *Safieh* down to Metemmeh and shelled that place, covering the advance of a foraging party. There were daily expeditions both by the river in the steamer, and by land, to get goats and cattle, vegetables for the sick, and green-stuff for the camels, which had already eaten up all the vegetation about the camp. We weighed anchor daily at 6 a.m., taking a party of twenty picked shots from one of the regiments. Small parties of riflemen used to fire at us from the left bank, but we had no casualties.

All the villages in the neighbourhood were deserted; but there was nothing to be taken from them except a few beans and lentils, and the native wooden bedsteads. A good deal of long-range sniping went on, but no one was the worse for it.

The British sailors and soldiers had trouble with the native bulls, which, docile enough with natives, resisted capture by white men. Nusri Pasha, the Egyptian, who had come down in command of the *Talahawiyeh*, was standing on the deck of the *Safieh*, watching my men trying to compel a recalcitrant bull down the bank.

"Let me try," said Nusri Pasha. "He'll obey me. You see."

And he crossed the plank to the shore, and went up to the angry bull. No sooner did the *pasha* lay hand on the rope, than the bull charged, caught the unhappy Egyptian between his horns, carried him headlong down the slope and into the water, and fetched up against the steamer with his horns fixed in the sponson, while Nusri disappeared into the river, the beholders yelling with laughter. The *pasha* was fished out, chastened but not much the worse for his extraordinary escape. Had he been impaled upon the horns, there would have been no more Nusri, tamer of bulls.

Every night the *tomtoms* beat in Metemmeh; and on the 28th, there was a great noise of firing, which we supposed to be the celebration of a religious festival. Alas, it was something else.

On 31st January, Colonel Talbot returned from Jakdul with a large convoy of supplies. He was accompanied by the second division of the Naval Brigade, which, it may be remembered, had not arrived at Korti when the Desert Column left that place. With the Naval Brigade came Lieutenant E. B. van Koughnet, in command, Sub-Lieutenant Colin R. Keppel (son of my old friend Sir Harry Keppel), Surgeon Arthur William May (now Surgeon-General Sir A. W. May, C.B.), and Chief Engineer Henry Benbow (now Sir Henry Benbow, K.C.B., D.S.O.). Never was reinforcement more timely; and it was with inexpressible pleasure that I greeted my shipmates. Once more I had officers; in the meantime, I had put the *Safieh* into fighting trim; and now we were ready for emergency. It came.

Every night I used to haul off the *Safieh* into the stream; and I slept on deck. Very early in the morning of the 1st February, I was awakened by a voice hailing the *Safieh*. I ran to the rail, and there, in the first light of the dawn, was a boat, and Stuart-Wortley's face was lifted to mine. He climbed aboard.

"Gordon is killed and Khartoum has fallen," he said.

Then Stuart-Wortley told me how Sir Charles Wilson's two steamers were wrecked, how his force was isolated up the river, and how the *Mahdi* might be marching down with his whole triumphant horde armed with all the guns and rifles of the fallen city.

"Then the soldiers had better run up more wire entanglements and earthworks as quick as they can. And I wish to God I had those two steamers!" I said.

I told Stuart-Wortley I would at once proceed to the rescue of Sir Charles Wilson's party, and sent him on shore to tell the news to Colonel Boscawen.

How the tidings came to the camp, is related by Lieutenant Douglas Dawson, who recorded in his diary how one "drew his curtains in the dead of night and told him"

(The diary was published in *The Nineteenth Century* for November, 1885. I quote from the copy kindly lent to me by the author):

February 1st. No member of our small force as long as he lives will ever forget this morning. Just at dawn I was woke by someone outside our hut calling for Boscawen. I jumped up and went out to see who it was, and then made out to my surprise Stuart-Wortley, whom we all thought at Khartoum.

I looked towards the river, expecting in the faint light to see the steamers, then seeing nothing, and observing by his face that there was something wrong, I said, 'Why, good heavens! where are the steamers, what is the news?' He said, 'The very worst.'

The full story of a very gallant exploit, Sir Charles Wilson's daring voyage to Khartoum, has been modestly and clearly told in his book, *From Korti to Khartoum*. The *Bordein* and the *Talahawiyeh* towing the *nuggar*, came to the Shabloka Cataract upon the day (25th January) after they had started. Here the *Bordein* stuck; and having been got off after many hours' work, she ran aground again off Hassan Island next day, during which the expedition advanced only three miles.

On the afternoon of the 27th, a man appearing on the left bank cried that Khartoum had fallen and Gordon was slain. No one believed him, because the air was full of false rumours, The next day, 28th, in the morning, a man on the right bank cried that Khartoum had fallen and that Gordon had been killed, two days before. No one believed him. But it was true. It was on that night that we in Gubat heard the guns firing in Metemmeh.

By this time, those in the steamers could catch a far glimpse of the roofs and minarets of Khartoum pencilled upon the blue above the trees of Tuti Island; and at the same time, a heavy fire was opened from the battery of Fighiaiha on their right hand. Then they came to Halfiyeh, where a battery of four guns fired upon them, on their left hand. The naked black men in the steamers served their guns with a furious zeal, while the British infantry fired steadily, and so through the smoke the red flags went on, safely past the point of the long island that ends opposite to Halfiyeh, the Soudanese ecstatically shrieking defiance and brandishing their rifles. At Halfiyeh were boats lying, and Khashm-el-Mus said to Sir Charles Wilson, "Gordon's troops must be there, as the *Mahdi* has no boats."

Then, from the *Bordein*, which was leading, they could see Government House in Khartoum plain above the trees, but there was no flag flying from its roof. As they passed between the island on their left hand and the mainland on the right, two more guns opened, and there began a heavy rifle-fire from both sides which continued for the rest of the way. Tuti Island, the upper end of which faces Khartoum, and about which on either side the Blue Nile stretches an arm to join the White Nile, was lined with riflemen firing over a dyke. At first Sir Charles thought them to be Gordon's men, and took the steamer nearer in, when the fire increased. So, writes Sir Charles:

> We went on, old Khashm protesting it was all up, and predicting terrible disaster to ourselves. No sooner did we start upwards than we got into such a fire as I hope never to pass through again in a 'penny steamer.' two or more guns opened upon us from Omdurman fort, and three or four from Khartoum or the upper end of Tuti; the roll of musketry from each side was continuous; and high above that could be heard the grunting of a Nordenfelt or a *mitrailleuse*, and the loud rushing noise of the Krupp shells. . .

They rounded the curve of the island, and there beyond the space of rushing water torn with shot, and the flash and smoke of bursting shells, Khartoum rose into full sight; and there, ranged on the sandy shore beneath the walls, the *Mahdi's* banners fluttered above the massed ranks of the *dervishes*.

All was done. Sir Charles Wilson had fought his way to the end, determined to go on till he was certain of the fate of the city. Then he knew; then, and not until then, did he give the order to go about.

At the word, as he relates, the Soudanese, who had lost all they had in the world, were stricken mute and impotent. Poor old Khashm-el-Mus wrapped his mantle about his head, crouching in a corner. They ran down stream through the fire, the Soudanese bravely returning it, the British infantry steady as ever, and won clear. During four hours they had been under fire. They ran down some 30 miles, and moored for the night.

The next day, 29th January, the *Talahawiyeh* struck on a rock in the Shabloka Cataract, and must be abandoned. The British were transhipped to the *Bordein*, the natives bivouacked on an island. Next day the natives were sent on ahead in the *nuggar*, hitherto towed by the *Talahawiyeh*, and the *Bordein* followed. The day after, 31st January, during the afternoon, the *Bordein* struck a rock, began to fill, and was run on shore upon a small island close to the large Mernat Island. When the accident occurred, Sir Charles Wilson was just preparing to run at full speed past the fort and battery of Wad Habeshi, which lay on the left hand some three and a half miles lower down. Mernat Island lies about 35 miles above Gubat by land, and nearly 40 by river.

Sir Charles Wilson landed guns, ammunition and stores. At first, he intended to make a night march down on the right bank; but he changed his plan and decided to remain where he was for the night.

Lieutenant Stuart-Wortley was dispatched to carry the news to Gubat in one of the two small boats, a *felucca*. He left at 6.45 p.m., taking a crew of four English soldiers and eight natives. They were fired at and missed by the Wad Habeshi Fort; and working splendidly, traversed the 40 miles in a little over eight hours, arriving at Gubat, as already related, at 3 a.m. on the morning of 1st February. Stuart-Wortley and his men faced death every mile of the way; and their voyage deserves to be remembered as a bold, determined and gallant achievement.

CHAPTER 14

The Rescue

And while lying near Metemmeh
He went—many a time you know—
Up the river in his steamer,
Dealing havoc on the foe;
And each gallant tar and Jollie
That was with him, fighting there,
Now would follow without question,
Let him lead them, anywhere.

 Songs of the Camel Corps (Serg. H. Eacin, R.M.C.C.)

(The men used to sing '*Our Navy on the Nile,*' of which the above is an excerpt; but the rest is so complimentary to the author, that he is obliged to omit it.)

At two o'clock in the afternoon of the 1st February the *Safieh* left Gubat to proceed to the rescue of Sir Charles Wilson's force. From the time the news arrived until we started, we were occupied in getting wood and stores. With me were Lieutenant E. B. van Koughnet, Sub-Lieutenant Colin R. Keppel, Surgeon Arthur William May, Chief Engineer Henry Benbow, Acting-Lieutenant Walter Ingram, Mr. Webber, boatswain, all of the Royal Navy, Lieutenant R, L. Bower, King's Royal Rifle Corps, and Lieutenant Stuart-Wortley, who had brought the news of the disaster.

The vessel was manned by picked men from both divisions of the Naval Brigade, and carried twenty non-commissioned officers and men, picked shots, of the Mounted Infantry, under the command of Lieutenant R. L. Bower. The engine-room staff consisted of Chief Engineer Benbow; two engine-room artificers, Royal Navy, J. T. Garland and G. Woodman; and one chief stoker, Royal Navy; an Arab or Egyptian engineer, and six Soudanese stokers. We mounted the two

Gardner guns in echelon on the platform made of railway sleepers and boiler-plate amidships, and one of the two brass 4-pr. mountain guns was placed in the turret forward, the other in the turret aft, both turrets being built of railway sleepers and boiler-plate, with which defences the ship had been cased above water.

The *reis* (native pilot) was stationed inside the barricade protecting the wheel, to guide the helmsman, who was a bluejacket. The native boats always carry two *reises*, one to look out, the other to steer. Our *reis* was mounted upon a box so that he could see over the barricade. In order to guard against the kind of accident which had befallen Sir Charles Wilson's steamers, I informed him that if he took us safely up and down, he would be rewarded, but that upon any indication of treachery he would be shot at once. He was then handcuffed to a stanchion, and Quartermaster Olden, with a loaded revolver, was placed at his side, Surgeon-General A. W. May, who very kindly sent me his recollections of the trip, writes:

> A quartermaster with the nickname of 'Punch' was told off to look after him, and he stood as grim as death at his side, revolver in hand, quite ready at the slightest sign of treachery to carry out his orders. . . I always attribute our getting up and down when the river was low and dangerous to your wise warning of the pilot.

The *Safieh* was simply a penny steamer in a packing-case. Where the packing-case was deficient, bullets went through her as through paper, and a shell would pierce her wooden jacket. The pinch would come when we sighted the fort at Wad Habeshi, which lay on our right hand, between us and Mernat Island, where was Sir Charles Wilson's party, and which was some 36 miles upstream from Gubat.

On 1st February we shoved along at the rate of 25 miles an hour, the most the *Safieh* could do against the current, stopped to get wood, and anchored in the stream during the night. It was impossible to navigate in the dark. The next day was almost entirely occupied in collecting wood, which was laboriously obtained by dismantling and cutting up the *sakiehs*, native water-wheels.

That evening we arrived within three or four miles of Wad Habeshi, and again anchored for the night. After weighing next morning, I assembled the ship's company and briefly addressed them. I told them that we were in a tight place, but that we would get out of it; that if we failed to rescue Sir Charles Wilson, the *Mahdi's* men would get them and would then come down upon Gubat; but that we would save Wilson's party. The men were as cheery and steady as possible.

At 7 am. we sighted Wad Habeshi on the starboard hand; and we saw, far up the river, the trees of Mernat Island, and the tilted hull and funnel of the stranded *Bordein*.

By 7.30 a.m. we were within 1,200 yards of the fort, and I opened fire with the bow gun. Wad Habeshi was a strong earthwork, with four embrasures, mounting four guns, and manned, according to Stuart-Wortley's report, by 5,000 riflemen. The only practicable channel ran within 80 yards of the fort. We could only crawl past the battery, and as we were defenceless against gun-fire, our only chance was to maintain so overwhelming a fire upon the embrasures as to demoralise the guns' crews, It was an extreme instance of the principle that the best defence resides in gun-fire rather than in armour; for we had no effective armour.

Accordingly, the starboard Gardner and the two brass guns, the 20 soldiers and 14 bluejackets, poured a steady and an accurate fire into the fort, disregarding the parties of riflemen who were shooting at us from the bank. There were some 600 or 800 of these, and one gun opened fire from the side embrasure of the fort. Poor von Koughnet was shot in the leg, and second-class petty officer Edwin Curnow, number two of the crew of the starboard Gardner, fell mortally wounded, and died that evening. But so deadly was the fire we poured into the embrasures of the fort, that the enemy could not fire the two guns bearing upon the *Safieh* while she was bore abeam of them. We passed the fort, and by the time we had left it about 200 yards astern, our fire necessarily slackened, as our guns no longer bore upon the battery.

Suddenly a great cloud of steam or smoke rose from the after hatchway. Instantly the fire of the enemy increased. Chief Engineer Benbow, who was standing with me on the quarter-deck, ran to the engine-room. A Maltese carpenter rushed up to me crying, "All is lost, sare, myself and my brother, sare! The ship he sink, sare!" and was promptly kicked out of the way.

I saw the black stokers rushing up from the stoke-hold hatchway. At the moment it was uncertain whether the ship was on fire or the boiler injured; but as she still had way upon her I ordered her to be headed towards the bank, away from the fort, and so gained another few yards. The carpenter's mate reported that there were three feet of water in the well, and that the vessel was sinking.

Then she stopped. In the meantime, our fire upon the side embrasure of the fort was continued by the riflemen; and it went on without pause, lest the enemy should get another shot in. I dropped anchor, and addressed the men. I told them that the vessel was all right, as she had only a foot of water under her bottom; that the stores and ammunition must be got up on deck in case she settled down; that no relief was possible; but that not a single *dervish* would come on board while one of us was alive.

The men were quite cool and jovial.

"It's all right, sir," said one cheerfully. "We'll make it 'ot for the beggars!"

Mr. Benbow, chief engineer, came to me and reported that the water must have come from the boiler, because it was hot; and that, as the shot which had pierced the boiler had entered above the waterline, the vessel was safe. I then countermanded the order to bring up the ammunition and stores.

In the meantime, the two engine-room artificers, Garland and Woodman, had been carried up from the engine-room, so terribly scalded that the flesh of their hands, forearms and faces was hanging in strips, like the flesh of a boiled chicken. They had been stationed by Mr. Benbow between the boiler and the ship's side, with orders to insert shot-plugs if the side was pierced; and in that position were farther from the exit than the Soudanese stokers, and therefore were more severely injured. The stokers were badly scalded. Two days afterwards, an odour as of the grave pervading the upper deck, a search discovered a stoker under the fortified superstructure. He was hauled out with a boathook, and was then still alive, although his flesh was peeling from his bones. He had resigned himself to die, as Asiatics will; and he died.

Considering the situation, I thought that upon the *Safieh* probably depended not only the fate of Sir Charles Wilson's party, who were isolated in a hostile country between the strong force at Wad Habeshi and the *Mahdi*'s host marching down from Khartoum, and who could not even rely upon the native soldiers with them, but the fate of the whole Desert Column; because if we failed to bring away Wilson, and his party were captured or slain, the enemy would be encouraged to descend upon the Desert Column at Gubat. I was, of course, at that moment ignorant of the movements of the *Mahdi*'s army; and could only conjecture that they were even then marching upon us. As a matter of fact, they were; but the exact sequence of events did not become known for a long time afterwards.

I asked Mr. Benbow if he could repair the boiler.

He replied, "I think I can do it."

He added that it was still too hot to examine. The time was then between nine and ten a.m. Mr. Benbow, assisted by the leading stoker R.N., who had been stationed on deck as stretcher-bearer, drew the fires and pumped out the boiler, when he found a hole some three inches in diameter, round which the plate had bulged inwards, its edges being torn and jagged.

By the time the examination was completed, it was about eleven o'clock. Mr. Benbow then set to work to make a new plate with his own hands. He had brought with him from the depot at Wady Halfa some engineer's stores: a piece of sheet-iron, and some bolts and nuts; part of the equipment I had brought from Korti, when General Buller asked me if I was going to mend camels with them. I remembered his chaff in that hour.

Mr. Benbow, with no other assistance than that of the leading stoker, had to cut a plate, 16 inches by 14, drill the holes in it to receive the bolts, drill holes in the injured boiler plate corresponding to the first to a fraction, and cut the threads of the screws upon bolts and nuts. The new plate being too thin to take the pressure, he also had to bolt an iron bar across it, drilling the holes through the bar, through the new plate, and through the injured boiler plate.

During the whole time he was below in the stifling hot engine-room at work upon a task demanding at once great exertion and the utmost nicety, the fire from the fort never ceased, Bullets pattered continually upon the hull, some of them piercing it, and striking the wounded men who lay below. At any moment another shell might burst into the engine-room. But Mr. Benbow went on with his work.

On deck, we continued to maintain a steady fire, hour after hour, upon the fort. It was our only chance. The slightest cessation, and they would bring their gun to bear on us. The range was between 200 and 300 yards. As we hung at anchor, the fort bore almost directly astern. It was therefore necessary to alter the position of our guns. A rough platform was built aft, upon which one of the Gardners was mounted, and where it was admirably served all day by Acting-Lieutenant Walter Ingram. Lieutenant Colin Keppel, in order to have room inside the narrow wood-protected casemate astern to train his brass howitzer, sawed off its trail.

The result was that after each discharge the gun leaped into the air and fell upon its back. After laying the gun, and before firing, Keppel removed the sight to prevent its being injured, and put it in his pocket. Keppel and Mr. James Webber served the gun all day, firing 150 rounds. The casemate itself was strengthened to take the shock of the gun by buttressing it with a stout strut of timber. At every discharge the whole crazy vessel shook and trembled; her plates started; and her bows opened. The fire from the Gardner and the rifle-fire, directed upon the side embrasure of the fort, were so accurate and incessant that the gunners of the enemy never had a chance, either to get their gun to bear or to remove it to another position. The few shots they fired travelled about 100 yards to the right of the steamer.

Meantime, Mr. Benbow, down below, went on with his work,

The noise of the engagement was so deafening and continuous that we did not hear the three shots fired upon Mernat Island, the signal arranged by Sir Charles Wilson with Stuart-Wortley to show that the party was safe; and we were so busy that we did not see the flags hoisted upon the wreck of the *Bordein* with the same object. At that time Sir Charles Wilson's party were themselves engaged with the enemy, who were firing upon them from the bank. Sir Charles Wilson was able to make out that the *Safieh* was at anchor and was heavily engaged. He then thought that we had the two steamers, the *Tewfikiyeh* as well as the *Safieh*, that one had been injured, and that the Safieh was covering her from the fire of the fort.

He immediately broke up his *zeriba*, embarked the wounded, some of the natives, the guns, ammunition and stores, and a small guard of the Royal Sussex, in the *nuggar*, and sent it down stream under the command of Captain Gascoigne. The embarkation was carried into execution under fire. Sir Charles then landed the rest of his force on the right bank (Wad Habeshi and the enemy were on the left bank) in his remaining small boat, a *felucca*. The whole party then marched down the right bank to a point opposite to the *Safieh*, Captain Gascoigne taking down the *nuggar* and the *felucca*. Sir Charles writes:

"As we got nearer, we could make out the white ensign flying bravely in the breeze, a pleasant sight for hard-pressed Britishers."

Upon the arrival of his force, it immediately opened fire upon the fort. I signalled to Sir Charles, informing him of the condition of affairs, and suggesting that he should move to a place lower down, where I would pick him up on the morrow. The *Safieh* lying some 500 yards from the bank, and Sir Charles having a difficulty in replying to my signals, Captain Gascoigne volunteered to go aboard. He took a native crew in the *felucca* and pulled across under a hot fire from the fort, which did not discompose him in the least. There was never a cooler man under fire than Gascoigne. He brought with him the two engine-room artificers of the Naval Brigade who had accompanied Sir Charles Wilson, and who at once went below to help Mr. Benbow to repair the boiler.

Captain Gascoigne returned with a message from myself to Sir Charles Wilson suggesting that, in order to divert the attention of the enemy from the *Safieh*, he should continue to maintain a fire upon the fort with a part of his force, while the rest proceeded farther down to form a *zeriba* at a spot suitable for embarkation; and that the women, sick and wounded should proceed in the *nuggar* during the night to the same place, to which I would bring the steamer on the following morning. Captain Gascoigne rejoined Sir Charles Wilson without casualty.

Sir Charles then sent Captain Trafford forward with the Royal Sussex, Khashm-el-Mus and most of the Soudanese, while Sir Charles himself remained with 30 men and one gun. They maintained a steady and a useful fire until sunset, when they marched after the rest of the party.

Meantime, Mr. Benbow, down below, went on with his work, It was about two o'clock when the artificers joined him, so that he had already been toiling single-handed, except for the leading stoker, for three hours. After another three hours, at five o'clock, the plate and bar were made, the holes drilled in them and in the boiler, and the threads cut upon the bolts and nuts. But the boiler was still so hot, that it was impossible for a man to be in it, and the plate could not be fixed, because it was necessary to pass the bolts through the plates from inside the boiler.

Mr. Benbow pumped cold water into the boiler and out again once or twice. We smeared a native boy with tallow, and I promised him a reward if he would go into the boiler. He was delighted. He was lowered down, to climb out again faster than he went in. After a short pause, he had another try. This time, in a frying heat, he stayed inside, passing the bolts through, while Mr. Benbow caulked plates and bolts and screwed them home. The boy was none the worse in body and richer in possessions than ever in his life. By seven o'clock the job was done.;

You can see what it was for yourself; for the plate is now in the Museum of the Royal Naval College, Greenwich. Rear-Admiral Sir

Colin Keppel (sub-lieutenant in 1885), writing to me on the subject, says:

> When in command of the gunboats under Lord Kitchener in 1898, on our way to Fashoda, about 300 miles above Khartoum on the White Nile, I again came upon our old *Safieh*, then again in the hands of the *dervishes*, with whom we had a short action. The first thing I did afterwards was to go down below (I knew where to look!) and found the patch which old Benbow had put on more than 13 years before.

Lord Kitchener afterwards had the plate cut out, and he very kindly sent it to me.

By ten o'clock that night, the boiler was repaired and the fires were laid. In the meantime, as soon as the twilight fell that evening, the fire from the fort slackened. It was my object to delude the enemy into the belief that we had abandoned the steamer; for, if they thought she was empty, they would not fire upon her, lest they should damage an invaluable prize. Moreover, did the enemy suppose that we were staying by the ship, they would during the night shift a gun from the fort, dragging it along the bank to a point abreast of the steamer; whence they could see the vessel looming on the water, whereas we in the steamer could not see them; whence the range was no more than about 80 yards; and whence a single hit would disable us.

But all depended upon our running the gauntlet in the morning. Therefore, in the hope of deceiving the enemy, as the darkness gathered, the four boats brought down to embark Wilson's party were ostentatiously hauled alongside, as if to take off the ship's company. Then all firing stopped; and after that thirteen hours' furious fusillade, the immense and crystal silence of the desert submerged us like the sea. Talking above a whisper was forbidden; every aperture was closed below, where the lamps were burning to light Mr. Benbow at his work, and no spark of light was allowed on deck. The men lit their pipes at a slow match burning in a bucket, and smoked under cover.

After leaving the *Safieh* in the afternoon, Captain Gascoigne had more adventures with his *nuggar*, of which by this time he must have been weary. It went ashore opposite to the fort, which of course shot at it, and Gascoigne must embark all except the badly wounded, under fire as usual. Luckily, the enemy failed to get the range. By sunset, the united exertions of Sir Charles Wilson's firing party had refloated the *nuggar*.

Late that night, we saw her drift past us in the darkness.

The fort fired upon her, but apparently without result, for she drifted on and disappeared. Then the enemy opened fire again upon the steamer. They had run the guns outside the fort in the interval, and fired a few rounds at us, accompanied by a heavy rifle fire. But the *Safieh* remained dumb and motionless. The firing ceased, the enemy evidently believing that we had abandoned the vessel.

I slept in snatches on deck, waking every now and then to look round. The officers were sound asleep, lying in a neat row on the deck. It occurred to me that, taking into consideration the position in which they lay relative to the gun on the bank, a single shot might kill them all. So, I roused them up very quietly, and bade them dispose themselves in various places. I remember how they waked with a sleepy grin, each looking for a separate corner, dropping into it and falling asleep again.

So far, our ruse had succeeded. At five o'clock the next morning (4th February) Mr. Benbow lit the fires, using the utmost caution, keeping the ash-pit draught plates almost shut, in order to prevent sparks, which would instantly betray us, from flying up the funnel. On deck, we were in suspense, all staring at the shot-riddled funnel. It kept its secret for fifty minutes; then suddenly it belched a fountain of hot ashes. It was then within ten minutes of daylight. Almost at the same moment a great shouting broke out in the fort, and a convulsive beating of *tomtoms*. Then the guns and rifles began to speak again.

What had happened was that when the pressure-gauge indicated 10 lb. of steam, the Arab captain of the stokers suddenly appeared at the engine-room hatch, and spoke swiftly in Arabic to his men, who, before Mr. Benbow could interfere, flung open the draught plates.

It was a close-run business. In the next ten minutes the steam had run up to 20 lb. pressure. Instantly we weighed anchor. The moment the steamer began to move, such a yell of rage went up from the *dervishes* in the fort, as I never heard before or since. Leaping and screaming on the bank, they took up handfuls of sand and flung them towards us. They had thought us fled, and the steamer theirs. And there we were, and there was the steamer moving away up river towards Khartoum; and the men of Wad Habeshi were naturally disappointed.

I took the *Safieh* about a quarter of a mile up stream, both to confuse the enemy and to enable me to turn outside the narrow channel, and at a comparatively safe distance. Then we went about, and ran down at full speed, again concentrating our fire upon the embrasures of the fort. Once more, as we came abreast of Wad Habeshi, we turned both Gardners and both howitzers upon the embrasures, in one of which we burst a shell; while the 20 soldiers and the 14 bluejackets maintained their steady rifle fire.

We were running now with the stream instead of against it, and our speed was the greater, and we stormed past the fort without a single casualty; and then, just as we thought we were clear, lo! there was Gascoigne's hapless *nuggar*, stuck and helpless some 400 yards below Wad Habeshi, and in full bearing of its side embrasure. As all depended upon the safe passage of the *Safieh*, I ran on until we were a mile from the fort and out of its range, and then dropped anchor.

I dispatched Keppel with six bluejackets in a small boat to the assistance of the *nuggar*. Rear-Admiral Sir Colin Keppel very kindly sent to me his account of the affair, based upon the notes made in his diary at the time.

> The riflemen, having got rid of the steamer, concentrated their fire on the *nuggar*. However, the range was long and their fire was not very accurate. After we had anchored you dispatched me in a small boat with six bluejackets to the assistance of the *nuggar*. After attempting to pull up to her, we found that the stream was too strong, and so I decided, having obtained your approval by semaphore, to land on the right bank, track the boat up until well upstream of the *nuggar*, and thus reach her. I found the only thing to do was to lighten her; and while Gascoigne and I were throwing overboard sacks of *dhura* and other things, I was struck in the groin by a bullet which went through my breeches but did not penetrate the skin. It only raised a bruise which made me limp for a few days. There was a considerable number of wounded in the *nuggar*. When she was afloat again, we drifted down. You got under way in the steamer and picked us up.

Such is Keppel's modest account of what was a very gallant piece of service on his part and on the part of Captain Gascoigne, who with their men were working in the *nuggar* under fire for three hours. Had they failed where they so brilliantly succeeded, the whole Column, as we learned afterwards, would have been jeopardised; for the steamer, returning to their assistance, would again have come within range of the fort.

The *nuggar* was taken in tow, and Captain Gascoigne's heroic strug-

"RUNNING THE GAUNTLET." THE ACTION OF THE "SAFIEH" AT WAD HABESHI, 10TH FEBRUARY, 1885.

gles with that unlucky craft were thus ended for the time. A mile below us, Sir Charles Wilson was waiting for us with his whole detachment. They were all embarked, and by 5.45 p.m. we had safely arrived at Gubat.

That night I slept so profoundly that I do not know when I should have awakened, had not first one rat, and then another, walked over my face.

Mr. Benbow's skilled and intrepid service had saved the Column with a piece of boiler plate and a handful of bolts. He received the special compliments of Lord Wolseley, who presented him with his own silver cigarette case; and was promoted to the rank of chief inspector of machinery. He ought to have received the Victoria Cross; but owing to the fact that I did not then know that the decoration could be granted for a service of that nature, I did not, to my great regret, recommend him for the honour. Mr. James Webber was promoted to be chief boatswain; and in 1887, his services being once more exceptionally recommended, he was promoted to the rank of lieutenant.

Surgeon Arthur May's services were inestimable. Always cheery, indefatigable and zealous, when he was not attending to the wounded under fire, he was on deck, rifle in hand, among the marksmen. It was a great pleasure to me to report in the highest terms of the conduct of the officers and men under my command, and specially to recommend Lieutenant E. B, van Koughnet, Sub-Lieutenant C. R. Keppel, Acting-Lieutenant Walter Ingram, Chief Engineer Benbow, Surgeon Arthur William May and Mr. James Webber, boatswain, and Lieutenant Bower, commanding the Mounted Infantry.

During the engagement with the fort at Wad Habeshi 5,400 rounds were fired from the Gardner guns, and 2,150 from the rifles. The figure for the brass howitzers is uncertain, the official report giving 126, but Sub-Lieutenant Keppel, who served one of the guns, mentioned 150 as the number fired from one gun in one day.

CHAPTER 15

The Effect of the Action of Wad Habeshi

The proximate result of the fight of the *Safieh* was of course the fulfilment of its immediate object, the rescue of Sir Charles Wilson's gallant detachment. But, years afterwards, it was made known that the full effect actually extended so far as to include the salvation of the whole Desert Column. In *The Royal Navy: A History*, vol. vii., Sir William Laird Clowes briefly mentions the fact, referring to Sir F. R. Wingate's letter to Lord Wolseley of 18th March, 1893. The passages in that letter to which he refers are as follows:

. . . It is therefore on these grounds only that I have ventured to collate evidence on an episode which may be considered to have been finally dealt with. . . . Moreover, with the light which this evidence throws on the situation, the results of Beresford's action cannot but be enhanced . . . that he was the means of saving Sir C. Wilson and his party is an admitted fact; but when it is realised that added to this, his action really saved the Column, it is, I consider, my duty to bring before you this evidence which, had it been known at the time, might have secured for Beresford and Benbow the greatest reward soldiers and sailors can hope to obtain. But late as it is, it may not be too late for the question to be reopened. . . .

In order to arrive at the actual details of the *dervish* movements subsequent to the fall of Khartoum, a meeting was held at the Intelligence Department, Egyptian Army, Cairo, on the 23rd February, 1893, at which the following were present, namely, Father Orhwalder, Kasha el Mus Pasha, Major Hassan Agha Mohammed (Kassala), Hassan Eff. Riban (late Maowin Berber

District) and present at Berber at that time; the Emir Sheikh Medawi (one of the principal *dervish emirs* present in the attack on Khartoum)....

In the unanimous opinion of the above Committee, the credit of having delayed the *dervish* advance and thus enabling the British Column to be retired safely is due to the action of Lord Charles Beresford at Wad Habeshi....

The following short extracts may be cited from the evidence which led the Committee to their conclusion. The first is taken from the statement of Esh Sheikh Murabek Wad el Tilb, a Kordofan merchant who arrived in Cairo on 30th May, 1888, from Omdurman:

... There were 3,000 *dervishes* there (at Wad Habeshi) under the Emir Ahmed Wad Faid and Sheikh Mustafa el Amin. These *dervishes* thought they could easily capture the steamer in which there were only about 30 men, but the English stood up and fought like men for many hours, they inflicted great loss on the *dervishes*, and forced them to draw off and disperse. Their chief *emir* was killed as well as their artillery officer.

The effect of this defeat on the *dervishes* was immense, and it also affected the whole situation. The survivors fled in many directions, spreading the news of the English victory far and wide....

If the *dervishes* at Wad Habeshi had succeeded in capturing the steamer, there is no doubt Nejumi would have hastened his march and would have intercepted the English before they could have got away from Gubat, but instead of that he halted when he heard of Wad Faid's death, and delayed some days in consequence at Wad Bishara and at Gereishab. He had a very large force with him ...

      (Signed)   Murabek Wad el Tilb

The second extract is translated from the German of Father Orhwalder, long a prisoner of the *Mahdi*:

.... It is an undoubted fact that Lord Charles Beresford's gallant action at Wad Habeshi was the means of saving the lives of Sir Charles Wilson and his party, who would have suffered a like fate to that of Colonel Stewart and his companions, and it is an equally undoubted fact that the *Mahdi's* success at Khartoum shook the fidelity of the Shagiyeh, but Lord Charles Beresford's victory at Wad Habeshi had the effect of making Nejumi dread meeting the English on the river, and decided him to attack them on the desert.

Lord Charles Beresford deserves the credit of having effected this and was thus the means of saving the entire British force.

(Signed)   Don Guiseppe Orhwalder

(23rd February, 1893)

It is obvious that the estimation of the conduct of the officers and men who fought at Wad Habeshi remains unaffected by the results of the action, which were neither definitely contemplated nor clearly foreseen. And the evidence I have quoted being irrelevant, strictly speaking, to any criticism of the action itself, is here cited, not in order to enhance the credit of the officers and men concerned but, for the sake both of its intrinsic interest, and for the purpose of illustrating, incidentally, the methods occasionally adopted under the system controlling the Royal Navy.

The effect of the action at Wad Habeshi exemplifies the extraordinary potency of the element of chance in war. Under what conceivable theory of tactics could it have been maintained that a penny steamer had the smallest chance of rescuing a detachment isolated in a hostile country, upon condition of twice engaging a powerful battery at short range, and twice defeating its garrison of sixty or a hundred to one? Or what self-respecting tactician would have predicted that in the extremely improbable event of success, its effect would have been to check, even momentarily, the advance by land of the main force of the enemy?

But the unexpected happened; and as it did happen, it would have been in accordance with a courteous precedent on the part of the authorities to have recognised the fact. I make no complaint of their action as regards myself; and only recall it here in the hope that no repetition of it will be permitted in respect of others perhaps less fortunate than I, The Admiralty refused to allow me to count my service in the Soudan either as time spent in command of a ship of war, or, as part of a period of command spent both in peace and war.

Their Lordships' refusal might have involved my retirement before I had completed the time required to qualify for flag rank. The Queen's Regulations ordained: that a captain must have completed six years' service, of which the first three years must be in command of a ship of war at sea; or that he must have completed four years during war; or five years, of war and peace combined.

After having been for over two years in command of H.M.S. *Undaunted*, I applied (in May, 1892) for permission to count the 315 days in the Soudan during which I was borne on the books of H.M.S. *Alexandra*, which were allowed as sea-time by the Admiralty, in the required five years of war and peace combined. The application was refused, on the ground that war service could not be reckoned by a captain unless he was in command of a ship of war actually employed in active service at sea.

Having completed my three years' service in command at sea, I applied (in April, 1893) for permission to count the 315 days sea-time, although they preceded the three years in command at sea, as part of the required six years' service. The application was refused, upon the ground that its acceptance was not necessary in order to save me from retirement.

A year and a half afterwards (in January, 1895) I repeated my application, pointing out that in three cases the Admiralty had, by order in council, conceded similar claims of admittedly much less force than my own, and that the only naval officers engaged in the Soudan war who were not allowed to count their time towards promotion were Captain Boardman and myself. Their Lordships then merely referred me to their previous answers, I may mention that my application was warmly and emphatically supported by Lord Wolseley.

CHAPTER 16

The Retreat

Upon the day after the rescue of Sir Charles Wilson's party, a court
of inquiry, under my presidency, was held to investigate the conduct
of the captains of the two wrecked steamers, and one of the *reises*.
The captains were acquitted. The *reis* was found guilty of treachery,
but his punishment was remitted in consideration of the fact that he
had brought Lieutenant Stuart-Wortley safely down the river after the
wreck of the *Bordein*.

The little *Safieh* was riddled with bullet-holes; she leaked like a
sieve, so that even before the action of Wad Habeshi, the pumps must
be kept going continually; and her bows, under the incessant concus-
sion of the guns, had opened out like a flower. The sides came away
from the stem, and in order to stop the water coming in, the natives
had stuffed rags and mud into the openings, which of course widened
them.

Upon our return to Gubat, I caused a dry dock to be excavated
in the bank; ran the bows of the steamer into it; closed it against the
water with mud; and kept two men baling out the water as hard as
they could go for eight hours on end, while we cut and fitted a new
stem and bolted the sides to it; a very difficult job, because the sides
of the steamer were rotten. The other repairs having been effected, I
took the *Safieh* (which was so decayed that the pumps must still be
kept going) out daily for foraging expeditions, to get cattle, sheep and
vegetables, and also to show there was fight in us yet. There were no
fowls, because the *Mahdi* had declared them to be unclean.

Captain Gascoigne and Khashm-el-Mus used to accompany me
upon these expeditions, Gascoigne taking command of the raiding
parties on shore: Lieutenant Robert A. J. Montgomerie (afterwards
Rear-Admiral Montgomerie, C.B., C.M.G.) was of the greatest service. Montgomerie was of extraordinary physical strength and prow-

ess, He joined me on 11th February, with Lieutenant G. W. Tyler, at Gubat. While helping to work the boats up the river, Montgomerie saved a gun which sank when the boat in which it was capsized. The weight of muzzle or breach (whichever it was) was well over 200 lb., and the water was shoulder-deep. Montgomerie picked up the gun, hove it upon his shoulder and waded ashore with it.

His exploits at Ismailia are still remembered. He was sitting in a saloon, where three French natives determined to provoke the English officer. They chose the wrong man. One of the trio upset Montgomerie's glass of beer, and although he did not apologise, Montgomerie, supposing him to have done it by accident, took no notice. A second man did the same, with the same result. Then the third hero deliberately threw down Montgomerie's glass with his hand. Montgomerie then acted instantly and with great rapidity. He knocked one man senseless, picked up another and threw him on the top of his friend, took the third and flung him up on the roof of the balcony.

Surgeon-General A. W. May reminds me that he and Montgomerie discovered, at some distance from the river, a garden wherein grew onions and limes. Montgomerie pulled the onions, while May collected the limes for the sick in hospital. But a lime-tree is armed with long and sharp thorns; and May, desiring to preserve his one and only uniform, stripped and climbed the tree in his birthday suit. Suddenly Arabs appeared; and May had but the time to descend, pick up his clothes and fly with Montgomerie back to the steamer.

Surgeon-General May also reminds me that upon another foraging trip, we landed a party of Gordon's Soudanese troops to capture a flock of sheep. Before the troops had time to get away with the sheep, the Arabs came down, and began to fire at them and also at the steamer. I sent a sergeant-major and a bugler to hasten the retreat of the Soudanese. Two of them, each of whom was carrying a sheep, lagged somewhat; whereupon the sergeant-major lay down, took careful aim, and fired at them. Neither he nor they seemed to consider the method unusual.

It was on one of these foraging parties that Quartermaster Olden saved the entire raiding party. Captain Gascoigne, in command of a wild lot of *bashi-bazouks* and the most of the men from the *Safieh*, had gone some little distance inland to a village. I was left in the *Safieh* with six men to serve the Gardner gun. The steamer was lying alongside the bank, but not close in; for it was necessary to keep a certain depth of water under her keel in a falling river, and to be able to shove off quickly. I had poles ready rigged for this purpose. The *bashi-bazouks*, who began firing from the hip at random with loud cries so soon as they came on shore, had vanished into the distance with the rest of the party; when I perceived afar off a crowd of *dervishes* gathering at a place at right angles to the line upon which the raiding party must return, and nearer to the *Safieh* than the village where was the raiding party. The *dervishes*, therefore, evidently intended to cut off the British force.

I sent for Olden, gave him his instructions, and sent him on shore with two riflemen. The three ran like hares through the scrub towards the enemy. They ran at full speed for about 600 yards to get within range. Then they scattered, concealed themselves and fired; moved again swiftly, and fired again; and kept on repeating the manoeuvre, until the *dervishes*, believing that the scrub was swarming with English riflemen, drew off; and the raiding party returned in safety. For this service, Olden was recommended by me for the conspicuous gallantry medal.

The black soldiers, going barefoot, used to come in with their feet transfixed by long thorns; these I cut out with a horse-lancet fitted to my knife; and the operation was like cutting leather. I had gained experience in performing it while getting the boats through at Wady Halfa. At Ismailia a more delicate operation fell to me. While fishing, my hook caught in a man's eyelid. The French surgeon who was summoned went to work with a lancet, and tried to pull the barb through the wound, causing the patient acute agony. I sent the doctor aside, and using one of a pair of breeches' bow-ties (for tying bows at the knees) drew the hook through to the shank, and severed it, much to the surgeon's indignation.

The expeditions up and down the river in the *Safieh* were amusing enough; but we were only making the best of the interval before the next move. Sir Charles Wilson had left Gubat on 6th February for Korti, where he arrived on the goth bearing the news of the fall of Khartoum, and a full account of the condition of the Desert Column. Lord Wolseley telegraphed the information to Lord Hartington (Secretary of State for War), who telegraphed in reply:

Express warm recognition of government of brilliant services of Sir C. Wilson and satisfaction at gallant rescue of his party.

Lord Wolseley, upon receipt of Sir C. Wilson's dispatch containing the account of the action at Abu Kru, fought on the 19th January, when Sir Herbert Stewart was wounded, had appointed Major-General Sir Redvers Buller to take command of the Desert Column, Sir Evelyn Wood being appointed chief of staff in his place. Buller had left Korti on 29th January, and had arrived at Jakdul on the 2nd February. Lord Wolseley had also dispatched the Royal Irish Regiment to reinforce the Desert Column. The Royal Irish marched on foot the whole way across the Bayuda Desert, each man carrying 70 rounds of ammunition, filled water bottles and rolled greatcoats.

The first detachment left Korti on the 28th January, the second on the 30th; both arriving at Jakdul on the 4th February. They left Jakdul on the 7th. Buller left on the following day; and upon arriving at Abu Klea, he left there two companies of the Royal Irish, the rest of which accompanied him to Gubat, for which place he started on the 10th. I saw the Royal Irish march in; a splendid body of fighting men, trained down to the last ounce, lean as hounds, and spoiling for a fight.

It will be observed that Buller was at Jakdul, half-way across the Desert, on the 4th February, on which date Lord Wolseley learned from Sir Charles Wilson of the fall of Khartoum. Lord Wolseley dispatched three sets of orders to Sir Redvers Buller in quick succession, the last reaching him at Abu Klea on the 10th, before he had resumed his march to Gubat.

Lord Wolseley's dispatch instructed Sir Redvers Buller to make every preparation for the evacuation of Gubat and the withdrawal of the Column. At the same time, its tenor left a certain discretion to Buller; who, replying to it in a private letter carried by the returning messenger to Lord Wolseley, "spoke," says Colonel Colville, in his official *History of the Sudan Campaign,* "hopefully of the situation." I think the presence of the Royal Irish, in magnificent condition, suggested to Buller that he could fight anybody anywhere.

In fact, when Sir Redvers came in to Gubat on 11th February, he wanted to remain and fight. At his request, I stated to him my view of the situation; which was, briefly, that unless we departed swiftly, we should be eaten up by the enemy, who were known to be advancing in immense force. I also reported officially that until the Nile rose, the two steamers remaining to us were practically useless: a consideration which proved conclusive. Sir Redvers Buller's dispatch, dated at Gubat 12th February, and addressed to the chief of staff, describes the conclusions to which he came after having carefully reviewed the situation (*History of the Sudan Campaign*—Part II).

The camels were greatly reduced in number and were nearly worn

FIELD-MARSHAL THE RT. HON. VISCOUNT WOLSELEY, K.P., P.C.,
G.C.B., G.C.M.G., D.C.L., L.L.D., O.M.
1833-1913

out; but if the column were to attempt any further enterprise, the camels must be sent to Jakdul and back to bring supplies, a journey which would take at least ten days. This circumstance was virtually conclusive. Sir Redvers adds:

> I regret to have to express now an opinion different to that which I expressed to Lord Wolseley in a letter dated the night of the 10th instant; but when I then wrote, I was not aware of the condition of the steamers and of the fact that the big one could not pass a sandbank 25 miles below this. Lord C. Beresford considers it doubtful if the other one can either. . . . Since writing this I am confirmed in my opinion by the news that Mohammed Ahmed (the *Mahdi*) left Khartoum *en route* here on the 9th instant.

In the meantime, Lord Wolseley had ordered the River Column to halt on its way. On the 10th, General Earle, in command of the River Column, had been killed at the action of Kirbekan. Lord Wolseley, until he received Sir Redvers Buller's account of the desperate condition of the River Column—deprived of transport, encumbered with wounded, short of stores (owing to bad packing), and without boots—retained his intention of effecting a junction of the two columns at Berber. At the end of the third week in February that scheme was necessarily abandoned. The River Column was recalled; and Buller, then on his way back with the Desert Column, was instructed to return direct to Korti.

On the morning of 13th February, the sick and wounded were dispatched with a convoy under the command of Colonel Talbot. Eight or nine miles out, the convoy was attacked, surrounded on three sides, and exposed to fire from the enemy concealed in the bush. Among the wounded were the scalded engine-room artificers; one of whom, recalling the incident in conversation with me recently, said:

"That was the first time my heart sank—when the bearers put down my litter, and the firing began."

After about two hours' engagement, when the convoy had lost eight killed and wounded, the Light Camel Regiment, under the command of Colonel Clarke, marching from Jakdul, opportunely appeared, and the enemy drew off.

Colonel Talbot (my cousin) very kindly sent me a copy of his diary, kept at the time. His account of the affair gives little indication of what was in fact a passage of very considerable danger. He was encumbered with a large number of sick and wounded; his force was small; the force of the enemy, though it was impossible to estimate the exact numbers, was formidable; and in spite of Talbot's skilful and prompt dispositions of defence, the issue must have been very doubtful had not the Light Camel Regiment arrived.

Colonel Talbot's account runs as follows:

February 13th,—Received orders from Sir R. Buller to march for Jakdul at dawn with 75 sick and wounded, Sir H. Stewart and the worst cases carried in litters borne by Egyptian soldiers from Khartoum. Escort of 300 men joined from the 3 Camel Regiments and about 200 Gordon's Egyptians from Khartoum.

February 14.—Marched at dawn 8 miles, and halted for breakfast. Outposts, just as we were about to resume march, sent in report of approach of large force of Arabs—mounted men, riflemen, and spearmen. The column was formed up, the wounded in the centre surrounded by camels lying down, and outside them the Egyptian soldiers. The Camel Corps troops were formed in two squares, one of the Heavy and Guards' Camel Regiments in front of the column, and the other of the Mounted Infantry in rear. Skirmishers were sent into the bush to feel for the enemy. The enemy opened fire and worked all round our force, apparently trying to ascertain our weakest point. It was impossible to estimate the strength of the enemy owing to the thick bush, but a considerable number of riflemen, supported by a large force of spearmen, were seen, and about 30 horsemen were counted. After the affair had lasted about two hours, and we had lost 8 men killed and wounded, the Light Camel Regiment on the march to Gubat appeared unexpectedly, and narrowly escaped becoming engaged with us, owing to both forces being unaware of the proximity of the other, and through the bush it was difficult to distinguish the Arabs from ourselves. No doubt the arrival of the Light Camel Regiment accounted for the sudden disappearance of the enemy.

It was Colonel Brabazon (now Major-General Sir J. P. Brabazon, C.B., C.V.O.), second in command of the Light Camel Corps, who, when the column had marched nearly half-way from Abu Klea to Metemmeh, went to his commanding officer, Colonel Stanley Clarke, and suggested that the Column should be immediately diverted to the scene of action. Colonel Brabazon led the column in the direction of the firing, and his two or three hundred camels made so great a dust that the Arabs thought a whole army was advancing upon their flank, and instantly fled away. The result was that, hidden in the bush, the Light Camel Corps occupied the ground vacated by the enemy, unknown to the convoy, which continued to fire at the place they supposed the Arabs to be. General Brabazon's account of the affair, which he very kindly sent to me, is as follows:

I halted the column, and the bush being very thick, the trees stopped most of the bullets; nevertheless, they were knocking up the dust at the feet of our camels, and a bullet struck my mess-tin. I ordered our regimental call to be sounded, '*The Camels (Campbells) are coming,*' '*Lights Out,*' and finally '*Dinners.*' But it was not until two or three of us pushed our way through the bush into the open, whence I saw the convoy preparing to give us another volley, that they realised we were friends and not foes, and precious glad they were to see us.

They had only a small escort and were of course hampered with the sick and wounded, and I think everyone who was there will agree that they were in a bad way. . . . I dined at the Guards' mess afterwards, and Douglas Dawson said that he had just given his men the range preparatory to their firing another volley, when he put up his glasses and made out the helmets and red morocco coverings of the camel saddles, and shouted, 'Come down! They are our fellows. Then, Dawson said, his soldier servant, who was standing behind him, remarked: 'Why, I could have told you they were our fellows ten minutes before!' I suppose he had recognised the 'Dinners' call.

So ended a comedy which had come very near to being a tragedy. Gordon's Egyptian soldiers, who were carrying the wounded, put the litters down when the firing began. Among the wounded were poor Sir Herbert Stewart, devotedly nursed by Major Frank Rhodes, Major Poë, Royal Marines, Sub-Lieutenant E. L. Munro and Lieutenant Charles Crutchley. Poë and Crutchley each had a leg amputated. All the wounded were lying helpless on the sand, listening to the firing, and moment by moment expecting the terrible *dervish* rush. A violent death was very close to them, when Brabazon and his men came in the nick of time. The convoy had one of the narrowest escapes in the history of the British Army. It remains to add that Colonel Brabazon received no recognition of his action of any kind from the authorities.

Colonel Talbot had been continuously employed upon the difficult and arduous convoy duty since the arrival of the Desert Column at Gubat on the 21st. Two days later Talbot started to return to Jakdul to fetch supplies. Not he nor his men nor his camels had a day's rest from the 8th January, when the Desert Column left Korti, till the 27th, when the convoy was back again at Jakdul.

The convoy reached Gubat on the 31st January; next day came the news of the fall of Khartoum; and the same evening the convoy marched again for Jakdul with sick and wounded. From Jakdul it returned with Sir Redvers Buller; arrived at Gubat on the 11th February; and started again on the 13th, as already related, with another party of sick and wounded. On the way back to Korti, Colonel Talbot, without engineers or commissariat, constructed a camp and built forts at Megaga Wells, where the main body, including the Naval Brigade, joined his convoy on 2nd March.

After Colonel Talbot's convoy had left Gubat on 13th February, I disposed of the poor old *Safieh* and the *Tewfikiyeh*, lest upon our departure they should be taken by the enemy. The six brass guns were spiked and thrown overboard, the ammunition was destroyed, the eccentric straps were removed from the machinery, and finally the valves were opened and the vessels sunk.

Then came the sad destruction of the stores for which we had no transport. The number of camels would only suffice to carry rations for three days, by the end of which the Column would have arrived at Abu Klea, where were more stores. When Colonel Talbot's convoy of supplies reached Gubat two days previously, the garrison had for ten days been living on short rations: nevertheless, more than half of what he brought must be destroyed. Count Gleichen (*With the Camel Corps up the Nile*) says that:

> 19,000 lbs. of flour, 3,000 lbs. of biscuit, 21,220 lbs. of beef, 900 lbs. of bacon, 1,100 lbs. of tea, oatmeal, preserved vegetables, coffee, and all sorts of stores were pierced and thrown into the river—(an example of waste in war resulting from deficient transport.)

Some of the medical comforts, small bottles of champagne and port, were distributed. One among us—I think his name was Snow—took a bottle of wine and swore he would keep it till he drank it in Khartoum. *And he did.* He went into Khartoum with Kitchener thirteen years afterwards, and drank his libation in the conquered city.

That incident reminds me that, when I went with the party of members of the House of Commons to Russia in 1912, a Russian farmer sent a note to the British admiral, of whom he said he had heard, together with a bottle containing mustard which he had grown, and which he sent as a token that the aforesaid British admiral would give his enemies mustard when he met them; for, said the farmer, the enemies of England would certainly be the enemies of Russia. I have that bottle of mustard.

What went to my heart when the stores were destroyed, was the dreadful waste of my drums of precious lubricating oil, carried so far with so great labour. My tears mingled with the oil as it was poured out upon the sand.

On the 14th February, at 5.30 am., the Desert Column quitted Gubat and started on the long return march to Korti, officers and men alike on foot, excepting the Hussars. There was hardly a pair of boots in the whole column. Some of the men cut up old rifle-buckets and tied the pieces with string to the soles of their feet. As for my sailors, they marched barefoot, every man carrying his rifle, cutlass, and 70 cartridges, and many of them towing reluctant camels. One camel to every four men was allotted to carry saddle-bags and blankets; and the camels kept dropping and dying all the way.

By the time he had been three days out, Count Gleichen, in charge of the baggage, had lost 92 camels. At first the weather was cool with a northerly breeze, and all started well. On the march, in default of water, I used to spread my clothes in the sun while I rubbed myself all over with sand; a dry bath that was highly cleansing and refreshing. On the 15th February we came to Abu Klea, somewhat weary.

We were of course in constant expectation of attack. On the next day (16th) the Naval Brigade occupied a sand redoubt, on which the two Gardner guns were mounted.

Sir Redvers Buller, finding that the water supply was insufficient and that there was not enough food for the camels, sent on the Soudanese troops, baggage, stores and camp-followers under escort to Jakdul, while he halted at Abu Klea to keep the enemy in check, until the unloaded camels returned from Jakdul, and until further instructions arrived from headquarters. The remainder of the column, entrenched at Abu Klea, thus became the rearguard, in the air, as the phrase is; isolated for the time being and deprived of transport and reserve stores; a dangerous position forced upon the general by the lack of camels.

In the evening began the customary desert performance, opened by the *dervishes* firing at long range from a hilltop commanding the camp, and continued during the long, cold, sleepless night with intermittent sniping to a *tom-tom* accompaniment. But our men were seasoned by this time; and although one among them was hit now and again, the situation no longer set a strain upon their nerves, but was accepted as part of the routine. That night two men were killed and thirteen wounded. It is true that the faithful José Salvatro, my Maltese servant, who had done and suffered so much, lost patience on this occasion. He was heating cocoa over the fire, when a bullet struck the tin and splashed the hot cocoa all over him.

"Why they fire *me*, sare?" said José. "Always firing *me*. *I* never did them any harm."

In the morning (the 17th) the enemy opened fire with a gun; which, after three or four rounds, was knocked out by the Naval Brigade with a Gardner.

I had walked a little way from the redoubt, when I was knocked over by a stunning blow striking me at the base of the spine, and lay helpless. I thought I was done; and I thought what an unlucky dog I was to have come through so much, to die on the way back from a wound in a place so undignified. But it was only a ricochet; my men carried me in; and I speedily recovered.

During the day Major F. M. Wardrop, D.A.A.G., and Lieutenant R. J. Tudway of the Mounted Infantry, with three men, employed the tactics I had used outside Alexandria two years previously. Riding swiftly from one point to another, and concealing themselves in the intervals, they impressed the *dervishes* with the delusion that a large force threatened them in rear, and so caused them to retreat. In the afternoon, Lieutenant-Colonel H. McCalmont arrived with the news of the action of the River Column at Kirbekan on the 10th, and of the death of General Earle. The mail from Korti contained a kind message of congratulation addressed by the *khedive* to myself, referring to the engagement at Wad Habeshi, as well as congratulations from home.

The total number of killed and wounded during the 16th and 17th was three men killed, and four officers and 23 men wounded. We heard on the 21st of the death of our beloved general, Sir Herbert Stewart, who, in spite of all our hopes, had succumbed to his wound on the 17th, during the march of Colonel Talbot's convoy, seven miles north of Geb-el-Nus. He was buried with full military honours on the following day near the wells of Jakdul.

On the 22nd February a convoy under Colonel Brabazon arrived with 782 camels. These were only just sufficient to move the stores and supplies.

It may here be noted that it was only a day or two previously that Lord Wolseley had received at Korti Sir Redvers Buller's letters describing the complete collapse of the transport of the Desert Column; and it was this information, together with a minute from Sir Evelyn Wood, who was at Jakdul, that finally decided Lord Wolseley to abandon his intention of combining the Desert and River Columns to hold posts along the Nile preparatory to an autumn campaign. At the same time, great anxiety with regard to the Desert Column prevailed at home.

Upon the morning of the next day (the 23rd) our picquets reported that the enemy had received a reinforcement of some 8,000 men and six guns. Perhaps the Column had never been in more imminent danger than it was at that moment.

Sir Redvers Buller discussed the situation with me. I expressed the opinion that the large force of the enemy would cut off our advance, rush us, and then move upon Jakdul and so on to Korti itself; and remarked that the column was short of transport and of provisions, and would be short of water.

"What would you do if you were in command?" said Buller.

I told him that in the evening I would light a larger number of camp-fires than usual, and, leaving them burning in order to deceive the enemy, I would then depart in silence and with speed.

"For a sailor ashore," said Buller, "you've a good head, I'll do it."

And he did.

At two o'clock the same afternoon, Sir Redvers Buller sent on his sick and wounded—32 of all ranks—with a convoy of 300 men commanded by Colonel Stanley Clarke; and that night, at 7.30, the rest of the column stole forth into the desert, leaving a ring of camp-fires flaming in the dark behind us. We halted after four hours' march and bivouacked in peace. Next day (the 24th) we were sniped by a few wandering scouts: and save for these, saw no enemy. Then began the three days' hard marching, on short rations, and very little water, in great heat, to Jakdul. Many of the men fell out: but not one man of the Naval Brigade.

We arrived at Jakdul on the 26th February. I did not keep a diary: but Lieutenant Colin Keppel's journal defines the situation in three eloquent words: "Water, mails, cigarettes!"

Next day I found time to write home, the first opportunity for so doing during the past six weeks.

Even now I am writing in a storm of sand and wind, my paper blowing one way and my helmet another, among my camels, who smell most poisonous. Poor things, they were eight days without water, and had only what food they could get when foraging in the desert. And they have so many and so large holes in their backs, that I am obliged to put shot-plugs in, to keep the water in when they drink. . . .

It was true that I put shot-plugs in the camels. My official report (and what can be truer than an official report?) contains under date 27th February the sole entry:

Employed repairing camels' sides by plugging them with oakum!

Lord Wolseley laughed when he read it. But although the surgery may appear empirical, it was wonderfully successful. The admixture of tar acted as an antiseptic.

On the following day (28th February) we resumed the march to Korti; on 2nd March the Naval Brigade joined Colonel Talbot's convoy at Megaga Wells, with the Heavy Camel Regiment and Royal Artillery. The Guards' Camel Regiment had gone on to Abu Halfa. The remainder of the column under Sir Evelyn Wood left Jakdul on 3rd March.

At Megaga Wells Colonel Talbot took command and we left for Korti, officers and men continuing to march on foot, very few having soles to their boots. There was one camel allocated to carry the kits of five men; 30 camels carried water; and 10 carried the sick. The thermometer registered 112° in the shade, and a hot wind blew. And so, we came to Korti on the 8th March, two months after we had left it.

Lord Wolseley inspected the Naval Brigade on parade; and expressed his extreme satisfaction at the work they had done, and the manner in which it had been performed. The next day the Brigade was broken up, and told off to different stations, under the command of Captain Boardman. I was ordered to rejoin the staff of Lord Wolseley.

Colonel Talbot notes that the Heavy Camel Regiment, of which he was in command, had marched about 850 miles; that the strength of the regiment upon leaving Korti was 23 officers and 373 men; and that its strength upon its return was 15 officers and 256 men,

Only four of his men arrived on camels. Not one of my sailors fell out during the whole way from Gubat to Korti.

Here, perhaps, it is not inopportune to place on record how delighted I was to work with the Army. We are really only one Service, for the protection of one Empire.

Nor, perhaps, to relate how that Her Majesty Queen Victoria, when she pinned the C.B. to my coat, said low:

I am very glad to give you this, Lord Charles. I am very pleased with you.

Her Majesty's words were my reward; for I will own that decorations as such have never attracted me.

I desire to record the excellent service of Captain F. R. Boardman (afterwards Admiral Frederick Ross Boardman, C.B.), who invariably did his utmost at the base to keep the Naval Brigade supplied. It was not Captain Boardman's fortune to be in the first fighting line, where is all the fun and where is often all the renown; yet the success of the fighting line depends entirely upon the energy, forethought and unselfish loyalty of those at the base of supply.

I happened to be discussing this point with a certain highly distinguished personage.

"We got all the credit," I said, "but not half enough was given to those at the base who sent forward the bullets and the grub."

"Grub? What is grub?" inquired the highly distinguished personage.

"I beg your pardon, sir. It is a slang term for food and provisions."

"So, grub is food, is it? How very interesting!" said the highly distinguished personage.

The sequel to our expedition was of course Lord Kitchener's masterly campaign. After the capture of Omdurman, and the blowing up of the *Mahdi*'s tomb, it was publicly stated that a certain officer was bringing home the skull of the holy man, intending to make it into an inkpot. The House of Commons (of which I was then a member) having nothing better to do, discussed the matter on 5th June, 1899. Lord Kitchener sat in the Distinguished Strangers' Gallery. Mr. John Morley (now Lord Morley) protested against the desecration of the tomb of the *Mahdi*. I replied to Mr. Morley, protesting against his assumption of authority in the matter. I said:

"Now I wish to take, most respectfully, issue with the right honourable the Member for Montrose upon this point. I say this with great respect and with great earnestness that, so far as I can judge from the right honourable gentleman's writings and by his teachings, he is no judge of religious fanaticism whatever. I say this with respect because, as I understand what he has written, he does not regard religious fanaticism as anything that can ever be powerful, because he says himself that he does not understand the question at all. That being so, I cannot accept the right honourable gentleman as a guide as to what should be done to check religious fanaticism. . . . The right honourable the Member for Montrose does not believe in the power of religious fanaticism. . . ."

Mr. Morley:

"The Noble Lord cannot have read my writings, or else he would have seen that fanaticism was one of the things I have written most about" (Hansard, 5th June, 1899).

A member said to me in the lobby afterwards: "You really ought not to say these things. Why do you make these assertions?"

"Because," I said, "I have read Mr. Morley's works."

"You know very well," said my friend, "that you have never read any of his books."

"I beg your pardon," I replied. "I never go to sleep without reading one of Mr. Morley's books, and I never read one of Mr. Morley's books without going to sleep."

CHAPTER 17

Sequel and Conclusion

For the first few weeks after the return of the Desert Column to Korti, we all believed that there would be an autumn campaign, and we looked forward to the taking of Khartoum. Lord Wolseley distributed his troops among various stations along the Nile from the Hannek Cataract to Abu Dom, there to remain in summer quarters. In his dispatch of 6th March, 1885 (Colville's *History of the Soudan Campaign*, Part II.), Lord Wolseley indicated the force he would require, and requested that the railway might be continued from Halfa to Ferkeh, a distance of 47 miles.

The railway was begun and was eventually completed. By 1st April the troops were occupying their allotted stations. One distinguished officer was so certain of remaining in his quarters, that he sowed vegetables in his garden. But upon 13th April Lord Wolseley was ordered to consider the measures requisite to effect a total withdrawal; and British faith was once more broken by a British Government.

By that time Lord Wolseley, to whose personal staff I was once more attached, had been to Dongola and had come to Cairo,

The news from home consisted chiefly of rumours of war with Russia; and I was gratified to learn that largely in consequence of my representations 50 machine guns had been sent to India. Machine guns were then upon their trial; and I had been consulted by the authorities as to their precise utility. We also heard of the hearty cordiality and enthusiasm with which the Prince and Princess of Wales were being greeted in Ireland upon the occasion of their visit to my country. There had been some misgivings upon the subject; and I had had the honour to suggest to the prince that if, as well as visiting towns and cities in state, he went into the country among my people and shot with them and hunted with them like the sportsman he was, he would find no more loyal or delightful people in the Queen's dominions.

As a matter of fact, neither in the towns nor anywhere else in Ireland, did the prince and princess receive aught but a most hearty welcome. Nor did the Nationalist party even attempt to arouse a formal demonstration directed against their visitors. They might have suggested, but did not, that some such conventional protest was due to the doctrine representing Ireland as a conquered country.

At the end of April Lord Wolseley and his staff, including myself, embarked in the s.s. *Queen* for Souakim.

The Souakim expedition under the command of General Sir G. Graham was then in full progress. On the 20th February he had been directed to destroy the power of Osman Digna, and to guard the construction of the Souakim-Berber railway. On the 2oth March, Graham fought the successful action of Hashin. On the 22nd was fought the bloody engagement of McNeill's *zeriba*. The British were surprised while at work upon the construction of the *zeriba*; the first shot was fired at 2.50 p.m., and the cease fire was sounded at 3.10. During that twenty minutes of confused and desperate fighting, some 1,500 Arabs out of an attacking force of 5,000 were killed. Desultory firing continued for an hour, when the enemy retreated. According to the official history, the British losses were 150 killed, 148 missing, 174 wounded, and 501 camels killed and missing.

The field of battle lay some six miles from Souakim; I rode out with Lord Wolseley to see it. Before we had ridden three miles in the dust and the glare of sunlight, the hot air carried a dreadful waft of corruption. The stench thickened as we drew near. A dusky cloud of kites and vultures hovered sluggishly and unafraid among a wilderness of discoloured mounds. The sand was heaped so scantily upon the dead, that lipless skulls, and mutilated shanks, and clenched hands, were dreadfully displayed. The bodies of the camels were mingled in a pile of corruption, clustered upon by the birds of prey.

And wandering about that charnel-ground, raking in it with a hooked stick, was a strange man whom I had met years ago in Japan, where he used to photograph the cruel executions of that country. He spoke no known tongue, but chattered in a jumble of languages; and here he was, equipped with a camera, and placidly exploring horrors with a hooked stick. Whence he came, and whither he went, we stayed not to inquire.

Day after day, for many days, the convoys of the expedition must pass and repass this place, which lay in their direct route, at the slow march of laden camels, and walking warily, lest they stepped ankle-deep into a festering corpse.

General Graham, having occupied Tamai, Handub, and Tambuk, dispersed the force of Mohammed Sardun on the 6th May; an operation which left him practically master of the district. But on the 11th May, Lord Wolseley, acting upon the instructions of the Government, ordered the general withdrawal of all troops from the Soudan. On the 19th, we left Souakim for Cairo. On the 27th June, Lord Wolseley turned over the command of the forces in Egypt to General Sir F. Stephenson, and with his staff left Cairo for Alexandria, there to embark for England.

Seven days previously (on 20th June), though we knew not of it, the *Mahdi*, who had given us so much trouble, had died in Khartoum. There he lay, listening perhaps for the footsteps of the returning English; for he knew that, although the English are ruled by people having the appearance of men but the ways of a weathercock, they may go, but they always come back. Thirteen years the false prophet slept in peace: and then the man who had sojourned in a cave at the wells of Abu Klea secretly collecting information, what time the Desert Column followed a forlorn hope, rode into the *dervish* city, and destiny was fulfilled.

Lord Kitchener of Khartoum fulfilled it, as strong men have a way of doing. A poet once said that the soul of Gladstone is now probably perching on the telegraph wires that bridge the desert where we fought to save Gordon, too late. I know nothing about that; but I know what the betrayal cost.

We learned afterwards that ere the *Mahdi* died, he had begun to concentrate his armies upon Dongola, a movement that was continued after his death, until the *dervishes* were finally defeated by General Stephenson, at Ginnis, on 30th December, 1885.

General Dormer had a way of his own with the *Mahdi*'s disciples. Addressing a prisoner, he said:

I suppose you believe in the *Mahdi* because he can work miracles. Can your prophet pluck out his eye and put it back again? Well, I am no prophet, but I can.

And with that, Dormer took his glass eye from its socket, tossed it in the air, caught it, and replaced it. The Arab was dumbfounded,

LEONAUR

ALSO FROM LEONAUR

THE FALL OF THE MOGHUL EMPIRE OF HINDUSTAN *by H. G. Keene*—By the beginning of the nineteenth century, as British and Indian armies under Lake and Wellesley dominated the scene, a little over half a century of conflict brought the Moghul Empire to its knees.

LADY SALE'S AFGHANISTAN *by Florentia Sale*—An Indomitable Victorian Lady's Account of the Retreat from Kabul During the First Afghan War.

THE CAMPAIGN OF MAGENTA AND SOLFERINO 1859 *by Harold Carmichael Wylly*—The Decisive Conflict for the Unification of Italy.

FRENCH'S CAVALRY CAMPAIGN *by J. G. Maydon*—A Special Correspondent's View of British Army Mounted Troops During the Boer War.

CAVALRY AT WATERLOO *by Sir Evelyn Wood*—British Mounted Troops During the Campaign of 1815.

THE SUBALTERN *by George Robert Gleig*—The Experiences of an Officer of the 85th Light Infantry During the Peninsular War.

NAPOLEON AT BAY, 1814 *by F. Loraine Petre*—The Campaigns to the Fall of the First Empire.

NAPOLEON AND THE CAMPAIGN OF 1806 *by Colonel Vachée*—The Napoleonic Method of Organisation and Command to the Battles of Jena & Auerstädt.

THE COMPLETE ADVENTURES IN THE CONNAUGHT RANGERS *by William Grattan*—The 88th Regiment during the Napoleonic Wars by a Serving Officer.

BUGLER AND OFFICER OF THE RIFLES *by William Green & Harry Smith*—With the 95th (Rifles) during the Peninsular & Waterloo Campaigns of the Napoleonic Wars.

NAPOLEONIC WAR STORIES *by Sir Arthur Quiller-Couch*—Tales of soldiers, spies, battles & sieges from the Peninsular & Waterloo campaigns.

CAPTAIN OF THE 95TH (RIFLES) *by Jonathan Leach*—An officer of Wellington's sharpshooters during the Peninsular, South of France and Waterloo campaigns of the Napoleonic wars.

RIFLEMAN COSTELLO *by Edward Costello*—The adventures of a soldier of the 95th (Rifles) in the Peninsular & Waterloo Campaigns of the Napoleonic wars.

LEONAUR

ALSO FROM LEONAUR
AVAILABLE IN SOFTCOVER OR HARDCOVER WITH DUST JACKET

ESCAPE FROM THE FRENCH *by Edward Boys*—A Young Royal Navy Midshipman's Adventures During the Napoleonic War.

THE VOYAGE OF H.M.S. PANDORA *by Edward Edwards R. N. & George Hamilton, edited by Basil Thomson*—In Pursuit of the Mutineers of the Bounty in the South Seas—1790-1791.

MEDUSA *by J. B. Henry Savigny and Alexander Correard and Charlotte-Adélaïde Dard* —Narrative of a Voyage to Senegal in 1816 & The Sufferings of the Picard Family After the Shipwreck of the Medusa.

THE SEA WAR OF 1812 VOLUME 1 *by A. T. Mahan*—A History of the Maritime Conflict.

THE SEA WAR OF 1812 VOLUME 2 *by A. T. Mahan*—A History of the Maritime Conflict.

WETHERELL OF H. M. S. HUSSAR *by John Wetherell*—The Recollections of an Ordinary Seaman of the Royal Navy During the Napoleonic Wars.

THE NAVAL BRIGADE IN NATAL *by C. R. N. Burne*—With the Guns of H. M. S. Terrible & H. M. S. Tartar during the Boer War 1899-1900.

THE VOYAGE OF H. M. S. BOUNTY *by William Bligh*—The True Story of an 18th Century Voyage of Exploration and Mutiny.

SHIPWRECK! *by William Gilly*—The Royal Navy's Disasters at Sea 1793-1849.

KING'S CUTTERS AND SMUGGLERS: 1700-1855 *by E. Keble Chatterton*—A unique period of maritime history-from the beginning of the eighteenth to the middle of the nineteenth century when British seamen risked all to smuggle valuable goods from wool to tea and spirits from and to the Continent.

CONFEDERATE BLOCKADE RUNNER *by John Wilkinson*—The Personal Recollections of an Officer of the Confederate Navy.

NAVAL BATTLES OF THE NAPOLEONIC WARS *by W. H. Fitchett*—Cape St. Vincent, the Nile, Cadiz, Copenhagen, Trafalgar & Others.

PRISONERS OF THE RED DESERT *by R. S. Gwatkin-Williams*—The Adventures of the Crew of the Tara During the First World War.

U-BOAT WAR 1914-1918 *by James B. Connolly/Karl von Schenk*—Two Contrasting Accounts from Both Sides of the Conflict at Sea During the Great War.

www.ingramcontent.com/pod-product-compliance
Lightning Source LLC
Chambersburg PA
CBHW021057090426
42738CB00006B/378